SAVING GRACE

John Cheeseman

THE BANNER OF TRUTH TRUST

THE BANNER OF TRUTH TRUST
3 Murrayfield Road, Edinburgh EH12 6EL
P.O. Box 621, Carlisle, Pennsylvania 17013, USA

*

First published in 1972 as
The Grace of God in the Gospel.
This revised edition first published 1999
ISBN 0 85151 772 2

*

*

Unless otherwise indicated,
all Scripture quotations are taken from
the New King James Version
© 1982 by Thomas Nelson, Inc.

*

Typeset in 12/13 pt Sabon MT at
The Banner of Truth Trust, Edinburgh
Printed and bound in Finland
by WSOY

Contents

Preface

This book is a revision of a work first published over twenty-five years ago. It arose out of discussions that took place in the day-to-day life of the Oxford Inter-Collegiate Christian Union. These discussions centred on concerns for the corporate life of the Christian Union and the presentation of the gospel to members of the University. Several of us who were students at that time were disturbed by certain man-centred emphases which had invaded the thinking and practice of evangelical Christians, undermining the biblical gospel of the grace of God.

When the Banner of Truth Trust approached me with an invitation to revise the original work, I was delighted to do so, because a survey of the current evangelical scene convinces me that the truths contained in these pages need to be given a fresh airing. Much of today's evangelicalism is dominated by the so-called 'feel-good' factor. Churches are no longer judged by their teaching but by their 'feel'. Biblical truth is being side-lined. Pragmatism rules over principle. Surely the great need of the hour is to return to the God-centred truths of the gospel and to gain renewed confidence in our Protestant and Reformed heritage.

I realize that in this book certain views are being opposed which are held dear by many a sincere

Christian. I recognize too that some will be wary of the sort of things said here, knowing that in the past unscriptural views have been based upon similar teaching, with disastrous results. There have been those who, starting from biblical doctrine, have constructed logical superstructures over and above what the Bible actually says, killing evangelism on the one hand, or minimizing their view of God on the other.

Let me therefore make it clear from the outset that I believe *both* in the absolute sovereignty of God *and* in the clear scriptural commands to preach the gospel. May I urge those who disagree with me to do so, not on the grounds of what they think is being implied, but of what is actually said.

In conclusion, I would like to thank several people for their help and encouragement: the Banner of Truth Trust, for their welcome invitation to do the work of revision; Mrs Donna Bourner, member of St James Westgate, who typed the manuscript; and last, but by no means least, my wife Joy who made sure that I had sufficient undisturbed time in the midst of a busy parish ministry! May the Lord God of Israel, who has visited and redeemed His people, be uplifted, glorified and worshipped in the hearts and lives of all who read this book.

JOHN CHEESEMAN
ST JAMES VICARAGE
WESTGATE, KENT

Introduction

This book is written out of concern and alarm at various things that are being taught and practised in the church today. The aim is simple: to present and expound the basic truths of the Christian gospel; to demonstrate these from the teaching of Scripture; and to show, in some measure, ways in which they are currently being diverted and mis-applied. This is not done from a wish to score points off fellow-Christians, nor for the sake of fanning theological fires, but rather from a reluctant but determined desire to re-assert truth that is in danger of being lost, and then to apply this truth to practical Christian living. The aim in charting rocks and shallows is not a perverse delight in them for their own sake, but so that ships may have a safe voyage.

It may help if I outline briefly the reasons why this book has come into being. They are basically two: one theological and the other practical. The first is obviously the stronger and would stand without the second, which, however, corroborates and supports it helpfully.

First, the theological reason. It has been said that whereas fifty years ago evangelicals talked of being 'saved', today they talk of 'making a commitment'.

That this is not just a trivial linguistic quibble can easily be seen as we examine why this shift has occurred. The implications behind the two words illustrate well the whole point. 'Saved' conveys the idea of man being rescued from a desperate plight, including the wrath of God and the consequences of sin. 'Making a commitment', on the other hand, not only loses sight of the basic life-and-death issues involved when a person is born again and brought out of darkness into light, but also makes the action and its effects the operations of man. The subject of the verb 'commit' is man: that of 'save' is undoubtedly God.

It would be foolish to suggest that all who speak of 'making a commitment' accept the implication which has just been stated. But this linguistic slide is symptomatic of, and gives us a clue to, a fundamental inversion of the gospel which is the cause of much current error. Basically, much present teaching in the Christian world puts the emphasis on man and his needs, his fulfilment, his commitment, his responsibility and opportunity. Without denying at all that man has needs, one of which is fulfilment, or that he needs to be committed to Christ, or that he is a responsible creature with opportunities before him, such a presentation is worse than a half-truth, and indeed positively misleading in that it has left out of the picture the Lord God who not only made man in the first place but also is the prime mover in the salvation of a soul. This is the basic reason for writing, and this book will consist of an examination in detail of what this involves.

The second reason, the practical one, is easily seen by examining current difficulties and points of weakness in the Christian community and by noticing the way in which they are traceable either completely or in part to teaching of this modern type. Not that this book presents an instant one-step cure-all: but the root cause of a problem must be the first step towards a cure. The symptoms of the problem are clearly to be seen. Our prayers tend to be very man-centred. Our love for the Scriptures is so shallow that we are content to skim through a passage like a careless lamb playing in a field when a wise sheep would be taking nourishment! We have no thirst to hear the Word preached, and in consequence some have given up expounding it for want of willing hearers. And – who can be surprised? – we have lost the vision for lost souls that characterized those days when men talked of being 'saved' and really meant it.

This has affected our missionary outlook and our ordinary evangelistic outreach. Would any of this be so if we all had the definite and thrilling knowledge that the Lord God himself had chosen and called us, without our deserving it, out of the darkness and deadness of sin – had forgiven us freely and was going to give us, through Christ, an eternal crown of glory – had given us, here and now, the Holy Spirit to live in us? What if this, which is no doubt head-knowledge for most of us, became heart-knowledge – burnt into us so that we could not forget it? Would we not then pray with gratitude and joy? Would we not be so filled with amazement and thanks for God's love that we would willingly go anywhere and do anything for Him? Would not our approach to the Bible be with eager reverence, delighting to be taught by it? Would we not gladly go into all the world – the next-door house or room, as well as the ends of the earth – to tell men and women of the incredible mercy and love of the Lord? But we do not – and it is hardly surprising. For instead of the grace of God we are used to thinking of the 'need for commitment'. Instead of salvation from sin and destruction we search for peace of mind and fulfilment.

The church is much given to talk of unity. However, there can be no real unity without truth as a basic presupposition, and it has been at those times when men have re-examined and re-experienced the basic doctrines of the Bible that the church has taken great steps forward. Conversely, when anything but the revealed truth of God as it stands in Scripture has been the foundation, heresy and division have rotted the whole building. This book is therefore written in the hope that it will play some part, whether large or small, in bringing the church, the company of regenerate men and women, more into line with what God has revealed in His Word. I sincerely hope and pray and this will result, by the working of God's Spirit, in great glory to His Name, in the devotion of grateful Christians and in the salvation of many.

Finally, some remarks on what this book is not. It is not a manual of theology, giving a full and systematic account of what the Bible teaches. Nor is it a personal credo. Nor is it a blueprint for a successful Christian organization or life. To hope to achieve any such ends would be futile: each community must learn to live in the light of the Word alone if it is to live as God wants it to. I am not pretending to have 'discovered' a new doctrine, or a new emphasis of doctrine. I merely wish to restate a very old, well-formulated doctrine, which finds expression, for instance, in the Thirty-Nine Articles and the Westminster Confession, as well as in such brief statements as the Basis of Faith of the Universities and Colleges Christian Fellowship (UCCF). So there is nothing new here. I am, rather, giving voice to a truth whose absence has been the indirect and direct cause of much that is at fault in current Christian teaching and practice.

The hope is simply to turn men's eyes back to what the Bible teaches, and then gently to suggest ways of current application. In so doing I will follow the example of the Apostle Paul in first setting out doctrine, and then turning to practical implications. This book is about the gospel, God's gospel of grace: and so I shall begin by asking some basic questions about this gospel and examining its fundamental points.

At the end of each chapter there are some questions which might be voiced by someone who disagrees or who has doubts about what has been said. There is then a brief attempt to answer each question, without intending to be exhaustive.

1

Biblical Foundations: God and Man

The aim throughout this book, but especially in these initial chapters, is first to find out what Scripture teaches, then to plead for heartfelt and unconditional acceptance of the truth which the Holy Spirit has sealed with His authority in His inspiration of God's infallible and inerrant Word. The 'faith which was once for all delivered to the saints' (*Jude* 3), for which we are commanded to contend, is that teaching which the Lord Jesus Christ left with His apostles. The possession of it is one of the marks of a truly apostolic Church. It is this doctrine and no other which I shall attempt to set forth in these chapters.

Nothing less than the full truth of the great doctrines of grace is the gospel of Holy Scripture. It does not matter whether this theology is termed Calvinistic, Augustinian or Reformed, since any system of theology stands or falls according to whether it is truly based on Scripture and in harmony with the entire content of God's Holy Word. The words of C. H. Spurgeon will bear repetition:

The old truth that Calvin preached, that Augustine preached, that Paul preached, is the truth that I must preach today, or else be false to my conscience and my God. I cannot shape the truth; I know of no such thing as paring off the rough edges of a doctrine. John Knox's gospel is my gospel. That which thundered through Scotland must thunder through England again.

To the question, 'What is the Christian gospel?', Martin Luther gives us an admirable answer:

Evangel is a Greek word, meaning glad tidings, good news, welcome information, a shout, or something that makes one sing, talk or rejoice. When David defeated the giant Goliath, there was a great shout, and an encouraging message was passed round among the Jews to say that their terrible enemy had been killed, and that they were free to enjoy liberty and peace; thereupon, they sang and danced, and made merry. Similarly, God's evangel, the New Testament, is a good piece of news, a war-cry. It was echoed throughout the world by the apostles. They proclaimed a true David, who had done combat with, and gained the victory over, sin, death, and the devil. In so doing, he had taken those who were enchained by sin, threatened by death, and overpowered by the devil; though they had merited no rewards, he redeemed them, justified them, gave them life and salvation, and so brought them peace, and led them back to God.

This gospel, the Evangel, which *evangelicals* love to proclaim, is a message which tells of One who turns rebels into worshippers; 'a proclamation of divine sovereignty in mercy and judgement, a summons to bow down and worship the mighty Lord on whom man depends for all good, both in nature and grace.' The gospel tells of the glorious triumph of God's life-giving, free and saving grace over the will of man which leads to his condemnation and death. This grace is that free and unmerited favour of God to sinners, by which God the Father loved us and had mercy upon us; by which the Lord Jesus Christ came to earth to die for our sins; and by which the Holy Spirit called us and drew us out of darkness into God's marvellous light. This is indeed good news; it is the very kernel of the 'whole counsel of God' (*Acts* 20:27) which Paul and the rest of the apostles did not shrink from declaring, proclaiming to the world the great work of the three persons of the Trinity in saving sinners.

God

The gospel begins where the Bible begins and where all true religion begins – with God Himself. The gospel is God's gospel; it is His power; it tells of His righteousness, His grace and His truth (*Rom.* 1:1, 16–17, *Acts* 14:3, *Eph.* 1:13). In short, the gospel is about God. Whenever superficiality, glibness, frivolity, stereotyped evangelism and similar things abound, while reverence, depth, personal desire for holiness, and overflowing love for the Lord Jesus are not very obvious, we may be certain that the root cause of the trouble is that the gospel that is preached is not the God-centred biblical gospel, but a new, man-made, man-centred substitute, like the one the Galatians sought after. The gospel we find in the

Bible is concerned with God. It seeks to glorify Him, and Him alone. This gospel causes men to fear God, love God, and glorify God; and any gospel which does not do these things is not the gospel which the apostles preached.

The God revealed to us in the Scriptures is *sovereign*. The first thing that the Bible tells us is: 'In the beginning God created . . . '. He is declared to be the sovereign Creator of all things, and this fact is made plain before any of His other attributes – justice, holiness, mercy, love – are revealed.

'Sovereign' means 'supreme', and God is sovereign because He 'works all things according to the counsel of His will' (*Eph.* 1:11), not out of necessity, but freely for His own glory. Creation was a sovereign act, because its cause was solely the good pleasure of God (*Rev.* 4:11, *Psa.* 33:6–9, *Rom.* 11:36). God's Word is:

My counsel shall stand,
And I will do all My pleasure (*Isa.* 46:10)

and to that perfect will, all things, and all men, are subject. 'I work, and who will reverse it?' (*Isa.* 43:13; see also *Isa.* 14:27, 2 *Chron.* 20:6).

In the words of the *Westminster Confession* (v:1):

God, the great Creator of all things, doth uphold, direct, dispose and govern all creatures, actions and things, from the greatest even to the least, by his most wise and holy providence . . . and the free and immutable counsel of his own will, to the praise of the glory of his wisdom, power, justice, goodness and mercy.

The fact that the providence of God extends to all things means that even human sinful acts are subject to God's will. This is the teaching of Scripture, as is clear from Peter's words at Pentecost: 'Him, being delivered by the determined purpose and foreknowledge of God, you have taken by lawless hands, have crucified and put to death' (*Acts* 2:23; see also *Acts* 4:27–28).

Here it is clearly shown that God's providence in no way lessens man's responsibility for his sin. So also Pharaoh was raised up in order that God might show in him His power, and manifest His name (*Exod.* 9:16); and while God says: 'I will harden Pharaoh's heart, and multiply My signs and My wonders in the land of Egypt' (*Exod.* 7:3), we also read: 'But Pharaoh hardened his heart at this time also' (*Exod.* 8:32). God is emphatically not the author of sin. According to His holiness, He hates it and judges it righteously. The almighty God revealed to us in Scripture is a God of whom it is said:

> He does according to His will in the army of heaven
> And *among* the inhabitants of the earth.
> No one can restrain His hand
> Or say to Him, 'What have You done?' (*Dan.* 4:35).

The final cause of all God's purposes is the manifestation of His own glory. In particular, our creation, redemption, sanctification and glorification were all purposed for the glory of God first and foremost (*Eph.* 2:8–10, *Isa.* 61:1–3, *John* 15:8). To the questions, 'Why did God create the world?', 'Why did He permit the occurrence of sin?', 'Why was salvation provided for men, and not for angels?', 'Why among those who hear the gospel do some receive, and some reject it?', there is only one answer which can be given: Because thus it seemed good in the eyes of God, for a more perfect revelation of His nature and glory. This is not to say, of course, that God has no concern for men in His dealings with them. Far from it! God is loving and kind to all men, as is clearly taught by Christ: 'Love your enemies, do good, and lend, hoping for nothing in return; and your reward will be great, and you will be sons of the Most High. For He is kind to the unthankful and evil. Therefore be merciful, just as your Father also is merciful' (*Luke* 6:35–36).

God's saving grace of course is the expression of even deeper love. God's love for His people is no less great or incomprehensible because it glorifies Him; neither are our feelings of joy and peace any less real and wonderful because they are the result of, and not the primary purpose of, our salvation. God's ultimate purpose in working all things according to the counsel of His will is not our wellbeing; yet we know that our highest good is the result of His providential care of His children (*Rom.* 8:28).

Let us pause here for a moment, and consider what has so far been said. To some, this doctrine of the sovereignty of God which has just been propounded may seem a little extreme; to others, perhaps, quite dreadful. To the carnal mind – to that old nature within us – the idea that man is utterly in the hands of God, to whom it belongs to direct his whole future, seems abhorrent; such a thought will not be countenanced at any price, for surely man is free to do exactly as he pleases? I will return to this problem later. For the moment, let me say that belief in the absolute sovereignty of God is required of all those who would seek to hold thoroughly scriptural beliefs, for this great doctrine is imprinted on every page of Holy Scripture from Genesis to Revelation. Although our reason and our natural inclinations might lead us to reject it or modify it, yet the truth is there, firmly embedded in God's Word. We are not bound to explain it. Martin Luther's dictum, 'Because God says so, I will believe that it is so; I will follow the Word, and regard my own thoughts and ideas as vain', should be ours as well. Nevertheless, let me suggest three reasons beyond the bare fact that the truth is in Scripture, for holding it:

Because the idea that God could be 'King of kings and Lord of lords' (*Rev*. 19:16), the One in whose sight 'all things are naked and open' (*Heb*. 4:13), and yet be a God to whom all things were not subject, is inconceivable. If God's nature is unchanging (*Mal*. 3:6) and His act of creation was a sovereign act, it follows that He is still sovereign over what He has created, being not merely its Creator but also its Sustainer and Ruler (*Heb*. 1:3, *Acts* 17:24–28).

Because it is pointless to claim and hold fast to the promises of God as given in His Word if they are made by One who is in fact *not* sovereign and therefore not sure of being able to keep them, being bound by the freedom man has been given, which He will never invade. No! The promises of our God are sure and steadfast and trustworthy. We claim them because their Author is our sovereign Lord Himself (*2 Cor.* 1:20, *Exod.* 12:25, *Psa.* 119:89–91).

Because prayer is reduced to mere wishful thinking if God is powerless to answer our prayers. It is pointless to pray for the conversion of a soul if God is not sovereign in salvation.

I am convinced that a right understanding of this truth about God is the fountain-head from which a right understanding about every other doctrine follows, and, more important, from which a right relationship between the sinner and his Saviour stems. Speaking of much modern evangelicalism, J. I. Packer has well said that its message

> conspicuously fails to produce deep reverence, deep repentance, deep humility, a spirit of worship, a concern for the church. Why? I would suggest that the reason lies in its own character and content. It fails to make men God-centred in their thoughts, and God-fearing in their hearts, because this is not primarily what it is trying to do . . . it is too exclusively concerned to be 'helpful' to man – to bring peace, comfort, happiness, satisfaction – and too little concerned to glorify God.

We are accustomed to hearing a rather glib 'All things work together for good . . .' whenever a disaster befalls. But due attention to the glorious truth set before us in Romans 8:28 should cause us to fall down on our knees in humble amazement and adoration before the great God who condescends to concern himself with every aspect of our lives:

> If then I am the Father,
> Where *is* My honour? (*Mal.* 1:6).

The God revealed to us in the Scriptures is, further, *holy, just* and *righteous*. He is a God who *reveals His wrath against sin, and judges it*. The holiness of God is incomparable and is exhibited in the law, and in the life and character of Jesus Christ (*1 Sam.* 2:2, *Heb.* 7:26). God requires of men that they should be holy as He is holy (*Gen.* 17:1, *Lev.* 11:44) and that they should obey the law, failure to do which is precisely the sin of mankind (*1 John* 3:4). The justice of God requires that all sin be punished (*Gal.* 3:10, *Acts* 17:31), the condemnation being borne, however, for those who are saved, by the Lord Jesus Christ (*Gal.* 3:13), while those who die in their sins are themselves condemned to eternal separation from God (*John* 3:36, *Matt.* 25:46, *John* 5:29).

Again, the God revealed to us in the Scriptures is *merciful and loving* (*Exod.* 34:6, *John* 3:16). If a man is saved, it is because of God's mercy in forgiving him his sins (*Eph.* 2:4, *Titus* 3:5). The God who is love, although He could justly condemn all mankind to death, yet has delivered from that condemnation a great multitude which no man can number, delivering them out of darkness and from the power of Satan, bringing them into His marvellous light, the Kingdom of His Son (*1 Pet.* 2:8–9, *Col.* 1:13). This is the mercy and the love of God toward sinners, the very heart of the gospel.

Richard Sibbes, commenting on God's title 'the Father of mercies' in 2 Corinthians 1:3, wrote:

Every thing is a mercy. And in every thing we take from God we ought to conceive a mercy in it, and to think, This is a mercy from God. If we have health, it is a mercy; if we have strength, it is a mercy; if we have deliverance, it is a mercy. It comes in the respect and relation of a mercy, all that comes from God. He is not said to be the father of the thing, but the 'Father of mercies'. There is a mercy contained in the thing. They come from the pity and love of God, and that is the sweetest. Therefore, He is said to be the 'Father of mercies' . . . The special mercy is forgiving mercy. If it were not for forgiving mercies, all other gifts and mercies were to little purpose . . . So the forgiving mercy leads to all the rest. Now these forgiving mercies, they are unlimited mercies, there are no bounds of them.

It may be objected that this discussion of God's character is unbalanced. So it is – I have dwelt at some length upon the sovereignty of God and said little about His holiness and love. This is intentional. My purpose is not to provide a complete theology of salvation, but rather to call to remembrance certain biblical truths which are frequently forgotten, ignored or misunderstood in these days.

Questions and Objections Considered

Many things occur which are against God's will.
The argument is this: All sinful acts of men and demons occur against God's will, for Scripture makes it plain that God is not the author of sin, nor does He connive at it, for He is holy; on the contrary, He hates

and abhors sin. But if things occur which are against God's will, He cannot be sovereign over these things. Therefore His sovereignty is not absolute, but limited in its exercise.

The fallacy of this argument lies in the ambiguity of the term 'God's will'. There is a distinction which must be made between God's decretive will and His preceptive will; that is, between His will which determines what He will actually do or permit as Governor of the world, which is a secret will; and His will expressed in declaring to His rational and responsible creatures what they ought to do.

Now, these are not always the same; *not* because God only pretends to want man to do good, having secretly planned that he should do evil, but because He sees and decides, in His wisdom and goodness, that it will be better – more to His glory – to permit and overrule sin for the accomplishment of His own purposes. So actual sin, while always against God's precepts, is never against His will in the sense of His decrees as to what shall come to pass; and He is sovereign over all.

These things are mysteries indeed, but they are to be accepted on the authority of God's Word. In the case previously discussed of the crucifixion, it is clear from Matthew 26:24 that God hated Judas' sin, and yet Judas' action was foreordained by Him. Thus it was that the Lord Jesus could say that He laid down His life of His own accord, no-one taking it from Him – that is, not against His will – even though man's sinful acts were a necessary means to that end (*John* 10:18).

God is made responsible for sin.

It is objected that, if God sovereignly overrules and ordains all things, then He becomes responsible for all events, and is thus responsible for, and in a real sense the author of, sin. This is contrary to Scripture, so God cannot be absolutely sovereign.

I agree that God is not the author of sin. Therefore His sovereignty must be understood consistently with this fact, and we may not say that He is the immediate or effective cause of any sinful action. When we say that God ordains a sinful action, this means that He is the cause of it only in a restricted sense, in that He decides to allow a responsible (that is, accountable) agent thus to act.

If it is said that God is responsible for sin even so, because He foresees the sin as a consequence of His direct action of foreordination, I reply that this argument is contrary to all common sense and human analogy. 'A righteous judge, in passing sentence on a criminal, may be sure that he will cause wicked and bitter feelings in the criminal's mind, or in the hearts of his friends, and yet the judge be guiltless. A father, in excluding a reprobate son from his home, may see that the inevitable consequence of such exclusion will be his greater wickedness, and yet the father may do right' (Charles Hodge).

If God is absolutely sovereign, why do we need to pray?

The fact of God's absolute sovereignty has a great bearing on the subject of prayer. Much current teaching on prayer would have us believe that God will not and cannot bring to pass His eternal purposes unless we pray. As one modern author puts it: 'The possibilities and necessity of prayer, its power and results, are manifested in arresting and changing the purposes of God and in relieving the stroke of His power.' Apparently, we are to believe that God's policy is shaped by the prayers of men. Sinful and corrupt human beings are able to change the sovereign purposes and plans of an almighty and holy God! Not only is this kind of teaching an affront to the honour and glory of our mighty Lord and Creator, it also directly contravenes the words of Holy Scripture:

> My counsel shall stand,
> And I will do all My pleasure (*Isa.* 46:10).

The God we worship is not someone who is constantly shaping His purposes and changing His plans as a result of the wishes of men, because with Him, 'there is no variation or shadow of turning' (*James* 1:17). 'I *am* the LORD, I do not change' (*Mal.* 3:6). God's designs and purposes are unchangeable and eternal.

But the inevitable question arises: If God is absolutely sovereign over human affairs, why do we need to pray at all? If it is true that 'of Him and through Him and to Him *are* all things' (*Rom.* 11:36), then surely there would appear to be no point in prayer. Yet, God tells us to pray: 'Pray without ceasing' (*1 Thess.* 5:17); and again, 'Men always ought to pray' (*Luke* 18:1). We read in James 5:15 that 'the prayer of faith will save the sick', and in the following verse that 'the effective, fervent prayer of a righteous man avails much'. The Lord Jesus Christ Himself was supremely a man of prayer. How then do we reconcile God's sovereignty with the need for Christian prayer?

We have seen that God in His infinite purposes has decreed that certain events shall come to pass, but He has also decreed that these events shall come to pass through appointed means. God has elected certain people to be saved, but He has also decreed that they shall be saved through the preaching of the gospel. In the very same epistle to the Romans in which Paul expounds the doctrine of God's absolute sovereignty in the salvation of men, he also stresses the vital need and responsibility for men to preach the gospel. 'How then shall they call on Him in whom they have not believed? And how shall they believe Him of whom they have not heard? And how shall they hear without a preacher?' (*Rom.* 10:14). The preaching of the gospel is the appointed means for the working out of the eternal purposes of God. Prayer is another means. God has decreed the means as well as the end, and among the means is prayer. And so, instead of prayers being in vain, they are among the means through which God fulfils His decrees.

The design of prayer is not to change God's will but to accomplish it. The Lord Jesus knew that after His death and resurrection He would be exalted by the Father. Yet we find Him asking for this very thing! 'And now, O Father, glorify Me together with Yourself, with the glory which I had with You before the world was' (*John* 17:5). The spirit in which we pray should be 'Not my will, but Yours be done' (*Luke* 22: 42).

We can now understand more fully the reason for so-called 'unanswered' prayers. God's answer and His will may often be the very opposite of what would be most acceptable to the flesh. 'If we ask anything *according to His will,* He hears us' (*1 John* 5:14). James says, 'You ask and do not receive, because you ask amiss, that you may spend *it* on your pleasures' (4:3). As we grow in grace and in the fuller knowledge of God, His desires will become our desires and our prayers will be in accordance with His will. 'If you abide in Me, and My words abide in you, you will ask what you desire, and it shall be done for you' (*John* 15:7).

> Prayer is not the requesting of God to alter His purposes or for Him to form a new one. Prayer is the taking of an attitude of dependency upon God, the spreading of our need before Him, and the asking for those things which are in accordance with His will; therefore, there is nothing whatever inconsistent between Divine sovereignty and Christian prayer (A. W. Pink).

A recognition of God's sovereignty should make us more, not less, zealous in prayer. It is because God has promised certain things that we can ask for them with the full assurance of faith. A true recognition of this doctrine will also result in a greater desire to worship and praise our sovereign Lord. Real prayer is an act of worship – an acknowledgement of His goodness, power and grace, and a submission to His will. Real prayer is coming into the presence of God and realizing our total unworthiness.

Prayer is designed by God for our humbling and for His glory. It is a means of spiritual blessing and growth in grace. To regard the purpose of prayer as simply our seeking from God the things of which we are in need is to consider prayer only from the human side. Prayer also needs to be viewed from the Divine side. 'Lord, teach us to pray.'

God's foreordination implies a denial of human responsibility.

Many of the problems arising in this whole subject spring from wrong or ambiguous definitions and ideas of determinism, responsibility and freedom. We must define terms carefully in order to make the distinctions which are necessary to a right understanding of these concepts. The doctrine of God's sovereign foreordination may be called determinism if by this is meant that whatever God foreordains must necessarily come to pass.

This is true. But it is not to be equated with fatalism, which makes fate control events in a way that is independent of secondary agents or causes. This amounts to compulsion. I repeat that foreordination is not compulsion, and man is therefore rightly called a free agent. By a free agent I mean one who is free (not subject to external compulsion) to do whatever he wishes. With obvious limitations, man is free in this sense. Clearly, therefore, God's foreordination is well and wisely adapted to the nature of man as a responsible free agent, and it encompasses man's will as well as his actions. To this there is considerable scriptural testimony (*Lam.* 3:37, *Prov.* 16:1; 21:1, *Jer.* 10:23, *Phil.* 2:13).

It may be said, however, that the objection is deeper than this. Granted that the absence of compulsion gives man freedom in one sense of the word, nevertheless, if foreordination entails necessity, then man is not free to act except as God has foreordained. Therefore man cannot be held responsible for his actions.

Agreed, man is not free in such an absolute sense as to be independent of God, but this does not mean that he is not responsible. Indeed, if it is said that necessity implies no responsibility, God's foreordination is not the only doctrine that must be rejected: His foreknowledge of events equally makes them necessary. Yet Divine foreknowledge is an attribute to deny which not only blasphemes the perfection of God but overthrows scriptural testimony, both direct and indirect. If God cannot foreknow events which depend on responsible, secondary agents, then He cannot cause men to prophesy such events: yet the Bible is full of such prophecies.

There is, then, no contradiction between necessity and man's responsibility, nor between God's foreordination and man's responsibility. Scripture demands that we hold to both.

Man

The truth about the nature of man is an outstanding example of the necessity to adhere faithfully to the overall teaching of Scripture, as it is here that a wrong understanding leads necessarily and logically to false or inadequate views about regeneration, the atonement, sanctification, and the whole plan of salvation. How easily this occurs, and how it is occurring all around us, will be shown in subsequent pages. For the moment, we shall concern ourselves with what the Bible teaches about this all-important subject. Man needs to see his situation in the right perspective. He is incapable of reaching a correct understanding of that situation intuitively. He needs to view it, so to speak, from the outside. As a fallen creature, he can obtain a complete and correct view of himself only by revelation; in other words, by reference to what God has spoken about him.

The teaching of Scripture is clear and unequivocal. Man is *totally fallen*; that is to say, the fall of Adam, in which all men participate (*1 Cor.* 15:21–22, *Rom.* 5:12–21), extends to *all* man's faculties (*Isa.* 1:5–6): his *heart,* which in Scripture denotes the very centre of man's being – the seat of his affections and personality, (*Matt.* 15:19, *Jer.* 17:9); his *mind* (*Eph.* 4:17–18); his *will* (*John* 5:40); his *conscience* (*Titus* 1:15); and every other part of him. Sin is described as being a *state* of enmity against God, and the transgression of His commandments (*Rom.* 1:29–32).

Since fallen men have no power of themselves to think, speak or will anything that may please God until they are regenerated and renewed by the Spirit of the Lord, all works done before justification have the nature of sin, as the Church of England Article xiii says. 'Those who are in the flesh cannot please God' (*Rom.* 8:8). There is therefore *not a single thing that a man can do* that will please God if he has not been born again. Every man, woman and child born into this world, with the exception of our Lord, is a slave to sin (*Psa.* 51:5, *Rom.* 3:9–20, *John* 8:34) and dead in sin (*Gen.* 2:17, *Eph.* 2:1), sins in all things

[23]

(*Ezek.* 21:24), and cannot cease from sin until God in his mercy delivers him or her from it.

The sinfulness of man does not consist solely of the voluntary sins which he commits, for these are the fruits of his corrupt nature (*James* 1:14, *Eph.* 2:2–3, *Matt.* 15:19). Empirically, we observe daily that sin abounds, but the Scriptures reveal to us that the situation is infinitely more desperate than we could ever have realized. Man's sin is not only what he does – which we can see – but what he *is*, which we cannot see as God sees it.

At this point, an objection may be made by some. If man is totally depraved and cannot but sin while, as I asserted above, God's providence rules the actions of men, does it not follow that man's sin is something that man cannot be held responsible for? Is not God, then, the author of sin?

These are important questions, and I will attempt to tackle them later. But a few remarks here will be appropriate.

It is noteworthy that Adam's reply to God, when asked if he had disobeyed God's commandment not to eat of the fruit of the tree of knowledge of good and evil, was, in effect, to put the blame upon God. 'The woman whom You gave to be with me, she gave me of the tree, and I ate' (*Gen.* 3:12). The unregenerate man, like Adam, attempts to cover his transgressions by objecting: 'Why does He still find fault . . . Why did you make me like this?' The answer of Scripture to such talk is: 'Who are you to reply against God?' 'Woe to him who strives with his Maker!' (*Rom.* 9:19–20, *Isa.* 45:9). We are not bound to explain these things, but to hold both to the impossibility of not sinning, apart from the grace of God, and to the fact that God holds man utterly responsible for his sin, and will condemn him, unless he flees to him for mercy.

The problems focus on what for centuries has been a theological and philosophical minefield, 'free will'. A common argument runs as follows:

God holds man responsible for his sin.

Man cannot be held responsible for something he cannot refrain from doing.

Therefore, man's will must be free to choose between sinning and not sinning; and hence, to choose between 'accepting' Christ and rejecting him.

I would assert that this conclusion is false, and highly dangerous, because of the falsity of the second premise, namely, that man can only be held responsible for what he has the *ability* to perform. I hold that this is false for two reasons:

First, because Scripture denies it. We have already seen that man's will, like every other part of him, is depraved, and *in bondage* to sin. Anything that is in bondage evidently cannot be free. Man's will, therefore, being part of a dead nature, is not free towards God in any sense, but is 'free' only to sin. Paul says absolutely: 'Those who are in the flesh *cannot* please God' (*Rom.* 8:8). Says Job:

Who can bring a clean thing out of an unclean?
No-one! (*Job* 14:4).

Neither is man free to turn to Christ for mercy. He cannot, of his own volition. The one thing that above all others, surely, pleases God, that thing over which the angels of heaven rejoice, is the sight of a sinner turning to God and repenting. Yet, men in the flesh cannot do this; it is impossible: God's Word says so. Notwithstanding, God commands and requires all men everywhere to repent of their sins (*Acts* 17:30), and He will judge them if they do not do so. God, who is righteous, will only judge a man for something for which he is responsible.

Second, because 'free will' and responsibility are different things. If by 'freedom of will' what is meant is 'freedom of action', that is, that when I do something I do it freely, without compulsion or constraint; then, it is agreed, man is a free agent, and is responsible, precisely because he is not forced to act *against* his volitions. 'Freedom' in this sense, therefore, means nothing more than the harmony that exists normally between a man's volitions and his actions. If I am forced at gunpoint to rob a bank, then I am not responsible for my action, since acted under compulsion, *against* my (law-abiding) volitions *not* to do so. Clearly, when a man sins, his *will* and his actions are united in sinning, and so man is to be held responsible for his sin. His volition and his action are both results of the corrupt nature which is his. But then 'free will' is a misnomer, and a misleading term to express the liberty of spontaneity which man does possess.

The notion that man is responsible only for what he has the ability to perform is utterly false. The fact that sinful actions spring inevitably from a sinful nature is no excuse; it rather aggravates the guilt. For man's sinful nature is no part of God's original creation, and man's duty (by which responsibility is to be judged) is determined by God's moral law, which unfallen man could keep. The fall and its consequences do not lessen our responsibility; they increase it. Our sin in Adam (*Rom.* 5:12–21) has made us unable to do good, yet the sinner, each one of us, is accountable to God in thought, word and deed, in every respect. God commands us to render complete obedience and satisfaction to the moral law of the Ten Commandments. That we cannot do so is patently obvious. Nevertheless, it is required.

Therefore man in all his faculties is as chained in the darkness of his sins, in captivity to Satan, as Peter was when bound by Herod on the eve of his intended execution (*Acts* 12); as dead as Lazarus in the tomb (*John* 11); as blind as the man Jesus healed (*John* 9). We must be on our guard against the theory that man's will is free, and not bound or corrupted – and, hence, that man *can* please God, if he wills to do so. Scripture is against such a theory.

We have seen that man is responsible for his sin and is under the condemnation of God. Even if man offended in only one part of the law, he would be under sentence of death, for, 'Cursed is everyone who does not continue in all things which are written in the book of the law, to do them' (*Gal.* 3:10). That condemnation which, but for the mercy of God, would be the just deserts of each one of us is declared in Scripture to entail a place of torment, of weeping and gnashing of teeth, of everlasting fire, of eternal separation from God (*Rev.* 14:10–11, *Matt.* 24:51, *Matt.* 25:41, *Matt.* 3:12, *Rev.* 21:8). These are truths about which we hear little, yet the Word of God plainly declares them. Scripture knows nothing of universal salvation, or of the annihilation of the wicked, or of purgatory, or of a second chance after death. The truth set before us is one of condemnation to eternal punishment. The plight of man, therefore, is truly dreadful. Unless he repents of his sin and believes in the Lord Jesus Christ, he is heading straight for hell. God commands, exhorts, beseeches him to repent and believe in order that his soul might be saved. Yet man cannot and will not do so. He is 'Fast bound in sin and nature's night', unable to lift a finger towards the attainment of his salvation. Yet only as he sees himself shut in between the condemning finger of the law, which shows him to be a miserable sinner, and the command of God to flee from his sin and lay hold of Christ, which he cannot obey (*Rom.* 2:8–12, *John* 6:44), does he see his true condition and consequently the direction from which deliverance must come.

Questions and Objections Considered

Experience shows that man can do and will do that which is good.

The doctrine of total depravity is not that every man is as bad as he could possibly be, but that man's nature is corrupted and disabled in every part and aspect – his mind and will as well as his body, affections, and so on. So we do not deny that the natural man is capable of doing and willing things which are in themselves good. This is an effect of God's 'common grace', that is, the work of the Holy Spirit in restraining men from sin and in leading them to do good, which extends to all men. Such grace is necessary to prevent the world from sinking into a condition as evil as hell itself; yet it is not the same as saving grace, and the good which results is in spite of the sinner's corrupt nature.

These good deeds are not acceptable to God, because they are without the only motives with which God is pleased – love to God and humble faith in Christ (*Heb.* 11:6). When the Pharisaical Jews kept every outward commandment of the law, God was not pleased with them because every act was marred by the sinful enmity of their hearts (*Jer.* 17:9). Their best deeds were as filthy rags in the sight of our Holy God (*Isa.* 64:6). God will not hear the prayers of the wicked (*Isa.* 59:2). The unsaved man may do good works in order to enhance his reputation, or to justify himself before God or man, or to quieten his conscience and silence the pangs of conviction of sin, or from the working of the common grace of God in him. But he will *never* do good works to glorify God from a grateful, penitent heart, for it is against his corrupt nature. Can a bad tree bear good fruit (*Luke* 6:43–45)?

The commands of Scripture imply ability.
The commands of Scripture imply moral *responsibility or duty*; but in no way does 'I ought' imply 'I can'.

If man's inability to obey the commands of the law were due to some natural or physical cause, he would indeed lack responsibility, and there would be no point in commanding him to do that of which he is absolutely incapable. But 'as the inability of the sinner to repent and believe, to love God and to lead a holy life, does not arise from the limitation of his nature as a creature (as is the case with idiots or brutes); nor from the want of the requisite faculties or capacity, but simply from the corruption of our nature, it follows that it does not exonerate him from the obligation to be and to do all that God requires' (Charles Hodge). A sinful nature imposes a moral inability as inflexible as prison bars, yet the sinner is responsible to do that which his own fallen nature renders impossible. If it were not so, a man would become less and less responsible as he became more and more sinful, an absurd conclusion which would make the punishment of Satan quite unjust.

It is worth adding that there *is* a point in commanding sinners to obey, even though they cannot do so. For through the law comes discovery of sin in all its sinfulness (*Rom.* 7:13). The sinner who realizes his condition, his guilt under the law, may be driven by the Holy Spirit to Christ for refuge. It is just as when Christ called, 'Lazarus, come forth!' Lazarus was dead; he could not obey; yet in that instant he was quickened by the power of God and came forth (*John* 11:43–44).

A closely related argument is to say that responsibility for sin implies that one could have avoided sinning. No, responsibility for sin implies that one *ought* not to have sinned. When the unregenerate man sins, he does so freely, as a free agent, and in accordance with his own wishes; and it is this which makes him responsible. It is true that his action is doubly necessary; necessary as all events are because foreordained of God; and necessary because of the corruption of his enslaved nature – but this in no way limits his responsibility.

2

The Way of Salvation

We will now consider how the redemption accomplished at the cross of Golgotha is *applied* to the individual; in other words, how, according to Scripture, man is saved.

A revealing example of the character of men under the dominion of Satan and in their natural state is provided by the madman of Gadara who, 'When he saw Jesus . . . cried out, fell down before Him, and with a loud voice said "What have I to do with You, Jesus, Son of the Most High God?"', and by the local inhabitants who, when Jesus had performed the miracle, begged Him to leave them (*Luke* 8:28, 37). Because the carnal mind is hostile to God (*Rom.* 8:7), spiritual things are hateful to them.

They cannot will to be saved, because their wills are 'ruled over by the iron lusts of their own hearts'. Never was this more forcefully expressed than by the Lord Jesus himself: 'You are not willing to come to Me that you may have life' (*John* 5:40; see also *Matt.* 23:37), an eloquent expression of the fallen state of man. The condemnation is that, because of his plunge into sin, man is *un*willing to lay hold of eternal life. The gospel says: 'Whoever desires, let him take the water of life freely' (*Rev.* 22:17), while sinful man testifies to a universal 'whoever does not desire'! It is evident, then, that, far from the Lord Jesus Christ waiting patiently and impotently at the door of our life for us to make up our minds to let him in, if left to our 'free will' we would be for ever lost and no-one could be saved. Yet God, in his mercy, *delivers, saves* sinners from that death, by drawing them to Himself. This is the work of the Holy Spirit, the Lord and Giver of Life, a work of *irresistible grace,* an *effectual call,* by which a man embraces the salvation Christ has won for him and by which he is truly born again of the Spirit of God. 'No one can come to Me' (because of his hardness of heart, and sinful unwillingness) 'unless the Father who sent Me draws him' (*John* 6:44).

The gospel command to repent and believe in Jesus Christ is addressed to all, without exception. The gracious invitations of the Lord Jesus Christ are without any restriction: 'Come to Me, all *you* who labour and are heavy laden . . . ' (*Matt.* 11:28; see also John 7:37). Manifestly, not all men do come to Jesus Christ, as He himself said (*John* 5:40), owing to their unwillingness; yet He testifies that in salvation, as in all other things, God is sovereign: 'All that the Father gives Me will come to Me, and the one who comes to Me I will by no means cast out' (*John* 6:37). Those who come to Christ do so because they have been *drawn* by the Holy Spirit and given new life by him. 'The letter [that is, the law] kills, but the Spirit gives life' (*2 Cor.* 3:6). Regeneration, the new birth, *must* then be wholly the work of the Holy Spirit. A man can no more assist, or will, his regeneration than he can his natural birth, or than a dead man such as Lazarus can assist in his resurrection. Man's natural inclination is to resist the Holy Spirit's work (*Acts* 7:51), and if the words 'new birth' and the entire metaphor have any meaning at all they signify that, although a man must be born again – and unless he is born of the Spirit he cannot see the Kingdom of God – yet it is totally outside his power to effect, to will or to desire the new birth. What man has ever effected, willed or desired his natural birth?

Man, a helpless and hopeless sinner, is utterly at the mercy of the Holy Spirit, who is like the wind which 'blows where it wishes, and you hear the sound of it, but cannot tell where it comes from or where it goes' (*John* 3:8). This is the truth Jesus sought to impress on Nicodemus to rid him of the idea that he could be saved anywhere, any time, whenever he felt the need. We repeat that man's will is *not* free with respect to the things of God or his salvation; his will is in bondage to sin, for 'the natural man does not receive the things of the Spirit of God' (*1 Cor.* 2:14). Salvation 'is not of him who wills, nor of him who runs, but of God who shows mercy' (*Rom.* 9:16). '*Of His own will* He brought us forth by the word of truth' (*James* 1:18). We were born 'not of blood, nor of the will of the flesh, nor of the will of man, but of God' (*John* 1:13).

We are now in a position to see the dangers into which a wrong or inadequate view of the sin and corruption of man can lead us. No longer would it be true that it was 'not by works of righteousness which we have done, but according to His mercy [that] He saved us' (*Titus* 3:5), but salvation would be conditional on the free will of man, conditional on man allowing God to save him at his – a sinner's – pleasure. 'I will put My Spirit in you, and you will live' (*Ezek.* 37:14) is the biblical gospel of the grace of God which saves sinners just as they are, guilty, vile, helpless, deserving only wrath and condemnation. It is not the biblical gospel that makes salvation dependent upon what I do. This is salvation by works, for if my salvation depends on my choosing Christ, while He waits for my decision, then, by comparison with my neighbour who is not saved, I must have done something to achieve my salvation which he has not done; in which case I have cause for boasting, and my salvation is the direct result of *my* decision.

Such a theory is, unfortunately, very common, but this is not the New Testament gospel. This gospel is gloriously *free*; it is a gospel which proclaims salvation all of grace, a gospel which we can take to all men, however black their sins (*Eph.* 2:8). As long as salvation depends on man's will, it is a gospel of works, the gospel which the Galatians were in danger of adopting and which Paul repudiated (*Gal.* 1:8–9). The supposed gospel of free will seeks to bring it within the power of all men to be saved; the biblical gospel of free grace proclaims the impotence of all human activity, so that sinners cast themselves wholly upon the mercy of God for forgiveness.

Although the purpose of God in saving sinners can never be frustrated (*Isa.* 43:13), and those whom God effectually calls infallibly come to him (*John* 6:37, *Rom.* 8:29–30), the term 'irresistible grace' is a slightly misleading way of referring to the work of divine grace in the human heart; for this work of the Holy Spirit is precisely to remove the sinful will to resist Him, so that when a man is saved he comes to Christ willingly and joyfully (*Phil.* 2:13, *Deut.* 30:6).

But it may be objected: What has all this to do with the simple command of the gospel to repent and believe? The promise of eternal life is made to all who *believe* (*John* 3:16), so surely repentance and faith are necessary for eternal life, and so must precede the new birth?

That repentance and faith are necessary for salvation is clear from Scripture (for example, *Acts* 2:38, 16:31), and the gospel which the apostles preached, and which we must preach, was a universal call to repent and believe. But we deny that man has any more natural ability to obey these commands to respond to the call of the gospel than he has to obey the law. Man is far too corrupt to repent of his sins and turn to Christ, just as he is too corrupt to obey the law as God requires him. Scripture teaches that, while all who *do* repent and believe in the Lord Jesus Christ *shall* be saved, repentance and faith are gifts of God, and they *follow*, but do not precede, the new birth. However, as soon as the soul is born again of the Spirit of God, as soon as it sees His light and His beauty, repentance (turning from his former sins) and faith in the Lord Jesus Christ as a perfect Saviour well up in that soul as natural expressions of the new spiritual life. Repentance is a sure sign of new birth, for the loathing of and abandoning of sin can only come from the One who is without sin, who is Light. It is impossible that man, who is in darkness, could ever of himself repent of his sins. 'A bad tree bears bad fruit' (*Matt.* 7:17). But as soon as the heart of stone has been removed and the heart of flesh implanted, repentance and faith follow, for the man has been made a partaker of the divine nature. *God* grants repentance and faith (*Acts* 11:18; see also *2 Tim.* 2:25, *Phil.* 1:29), that faith by which a man is justified (*Rom.* 3:26).

The fact that this saving faith is the gift of God and the fruit of regeneration enables Paul to say: 'Where *is* boasting then? It is excluded' (*Rom.* 3:27). 'By grace you have been saved through faith; and this not from yourselves: it is the gift of God: not by works, so that no-one can boast' (*Eph.* 2:8–9). Man certainly would have cause to boast if repentance and faith were conditions, works he had to perform in order to be born again. But the gospel forbids it! God saves sinners who are on the road to destruction and unable to do anything about it, and this out of His mercy and grace!

It is important to understand clearly the *nature* of true saving faith. According to the gospel, it is the means by which the sinner appropriates for himself the righteousness of Christ and thereby is declared to be 'justified' before God. Faith is the holding out to God of empty hands in order to receive the white robes of salvation with which God has promised to clothe all who believe in his Son. But it is God Him-self who is the justifier of the ungodly; it is God who remembers no more the sins of the unrighteous; it is God who reckons the sinner as righteous on account of Christ's atoning death. In short, faith is nothing more than the means by which the sinner apprehends and receives the blessings that flow to him because of the eternal love of the triune God. With the exercise of faith the scales fall from our eyes and we claim the Saviour of the world to be our own.

We have seen that saving faith comes to us through the working of the Holy Spirit. However, although we ascribe our faith entirely to Him, we must not fall into the error of thinking that our justification is a *reward* for our faith. Romans 4 makes it clear that, if the latter were the case, then faith exercised in Christ would itself become a work, *meriting* acceptance with God; and the distinction between works that merit, and faith that receives, which Paul is so anxious to draw, would be confused. The crucial distinction must be drawn between the work of Christ *for* us, in obtaining our salvation, and the work of the Spirit *in* us, revealing that salvation to us and enabling us to receive it. 'Faith justifies us, no, *not even as a gift of the Holy Ghost,* but solely on account of its reference to Christ' (Luther). A few words of Brentius, writing to Melanchthon, under-lines the cardinal importance of this distinction:

> Justification comes to us neither *on account of* our love nor our faith, but solely on account of Christ; and yet it comes *through* (by means of) faith. Faith

does not justify as a work of goodness, but simply as a receiver of promised mercy . . . We do not *merit*, we only *obtain* justification . . . Faith is but the organ, the instrument, the medium; Christ alone is the satisfaction and the merit.

Justification by faith is the heart of the gospel. This is what is contained in the promise, 'Whoever believes in Him shall not perish, but have eternal life.' If we fail to grasp the fact that the righteousness which justifies us is *imputed* and not infused or inherent, we shall find that, in substance, what we preach is a gospel of works, not a gospel of grace.

A problem still remains: Why are all sinners commanded to come to Christ, to repent of their sins, when they are not able to do so? This is the same problem that we met before when considering and refuting the argument that responsibility implies ability. It is true that a man cannot come to Christ except he be drawn by the Father; it is evident that not all men are saved, and hence, that not all men are drawn; it is also true that the sin of rejection of Christ is a sin for which man will be judged, a sin for which he is therefore responsible (*John* 3:18–19, 36; 16:8–9). So the gospel command is addressed to sinners who are unable to help themselves. These are truths which we are unable to reconcile, yet the Scriptures require us to hold firmly to both, and to preach both man's duty to believe the gospel and his sinful inability to do so; to deliver the command to sinners to believe in the Lord Jesus Christ for their salvation and to proclaim that only grace can enable this. 'It is an axiom of theology that, if a man is saved, God must get all the glory for it; if he is condemned, God must not be blamed for it.'

This, then, is the biblical scheme of things:

1. Christ is willing to save all who come to Him for forgiveness. He commands all men to repent and believe.

2. Man is unwilling to come; he cannot repent and believe.

3. Man must be made willing to come; he must be made able to repent and believe.

Therefore, we must cast ourselves on the mercy of God, who alone can renew the heart and forgive sins. 'Believe on the Lord Jesus Christ' (*Acts* 16:31).

Questions and Objections Considered

Scripture speaks of resisting the Holy Spirit, showing that it is possible to do so; Acts 7:51: 'You always resist the Holy Spirit'; Eph. 4:30: 'Do not grieve the Holy Spirit of God'.

We do not assert that *all* the operations of the Holy Spirit are irresistible. On the contrary, it is the very nature of unregenerate man *always* to resist the Holy Spirit, as Stephen says. The Spirit sent prophets: men rejected them and killed them. He applies convictions of sin to the heart: men stifle them. He causes Christ to be proclaimed in the gospel: men will not hear.

Yet in all this the will of God is not overthrown, and in every case He accomplishes exactly what He intended. 'For who has resisted His will?' (*Rom.* 9:19). Conviction of sin itself has a tendency to conversion; so that he who stifles conviction resists the Holy Spirit. But in those whom He effectually calls out of darkness into light, He not only over-comes the resistance, He actually changes it into willing compliance.

Here is perhaps where the term 'irresistible grace' is misleading. For it is not that the sinner would like to resist but cannot because grace is too strong for him; no, that would be compulsion, conversion against one's will. Rather, when one is born again, the *whole* nature is changed, including the will, so that all resistance to the work of God vanishes and the newly-regenerate person gladly accepts and runs to Christ by faith.

We return to the questions, 'For who makes you differ from another? And what do you have that you did not receive?' (*1 Cor.* 4:7). Is it that we ourselves make ourselves different by our self-caused response to the Spirit's pleading? Or is the whole glory of our salvation to belong to God alone? The fact is that we were dead in trespasses and sins (*Eph.* 2:1). God alone can raise the dead to life, and we do not resist His resurrection power. If we could, we *would*, and not one of us would be saved.

This eliminates free will.
For once I agree with the objection! Yes, the idol free will, which pretends to direct the eternal destiny of mankind, is overthrown, and with it all grounds for human pride and boasting are cast down. Let us accept the simple, humbling testimony of the Scriptures that the grace of God does not depend on

man's will (*Rom.* 9:16), that God's children are born 'not of the will of man, but of God' (*John* 1:13). The doctrines of irresistible grace and of God's unconditional election destroy free will; just as David's stone, rightly aimed, eliminated Goliath, destroying once and for all the enemy of the people of God. 'Free will' is not a friend, but an enemy; for the will of man, being corrupt, leads to his condemnation; man's true friend is the free grace of God, which comes to his rescue, delivering him from the relentless tyranny of his own nature, from which he would otherwise be powerless to escape.

3

Salvation Planned

As I have tried to show, the Scriptures proclaim the absolute sovereignty of God. 'The Son gives life to whom He will' (*John* 5:21). 'It is the Spirit who gives life; the flesh profits nothing' (*John* 6:63). So, since we are unable, by reason of our sin, to come to Christ, since it is the Holy Spirit who effects the new birth in our hearts, since the purpose of God in saving sinners is always accomplished, and since all are not saved, it is God, and not man, who decides who shall be saved: 'Therefore I have said to you that no one can come to Me, unless it has been granted to him by My Father' (*John* 6:65). It was therefore the will of God that some should be saved, while others He saw fit, 'according to the unsearchable counsel of His own will . . . for the glory of His sovereign power over His creatures, to pass by' (*Westminster Confession* iii.7). This is the biblical truth of *unconditional election*.

It follows naturally from what has so far been said about the total depravity of man and the sovereignty of God. We who are saved are 'Debtors to mercy alone', and the God who has saved us is the One who 'has mercy on whom He wills, and whom He wills He hardens' (*Rom.* 9:18).

This is a hard truth, but then it is always hard to accept the humbling fact that God, and not man, ordains what shall be. After the words of the Lord Jesus Christ: 'No one can come to me, unless it has been granted to him by My Father', we read: 'From that *time* many of His disciples went back and walked with Him no more' (*John* 6:65–66). These sad words testify to the fact that the carnal mind constantly desires to assert itself against God in denying His sovereignty. As Spurgeon said, 'Many men cavil at election; the very word with some is a great bugbear; they no sooner hear it than they turn upon their heel for anger . . . But not all the sophisms of the learned, not all the legerdemain of the cunning, will ever be able to sweep the doctrine of election out of Holy Scripture.' And this is the reason that we hold this or any other belief, because it is scriptural, because it is a truth from God.

We have seen in the last section that the biblical principle is always 'Salvation is of the Lord'; 'The LORD kills, and makes alive' (*Jon.* 2:9, *1 Sam.* 2:6). Those whom the Lord, in His mercy, purposed to save are *known* by Him (*2 Tim.* 2:19) before they could have done anything to merit God's favour (*Rom.* 8:29). In the words of the Westminster Confession (iii.5):

Those of mankind that are predestinated unto life, God, before the foundation of the world was laid, according to His eternal and immutable purpose, and the secret counsel and good pleasure of His will, hath chosen, in Christ, unto everlasting glory, out of His mere free grace and love, without any foresight of faith, or good works, or perseverance in either of them, or any other thing in the creature, as conditions, or causes moving Him thereunto: and all to the praise of His glorious grace.

There are three important things to notice about election:

Its source. It is God's purpose (*Eph.* 1:9–11, *2 Tim.* 1:9, *Rom.* 8:28). Spurgeon, preaching on Galatians 1:15, said:

You will perceive, I think, in these words, that the divine plan of salvation is very clearly laid down. It begins, you see, with the will and pleasure of God. 'When it pleased God . . .'. The foundation of salvation is not laid in the will of man. It does not begin with man's obedience, and then proceed onward to the purpose of God, but here, in the purpose of God, is its commencement; here is the fountainhead from which the living waters flow.

Its nature. It is unconditional. God set us apart for Himself at the very beginning (*Eph.* 1:4), not according to His foresight of anything in us meriting our election (such as faith, or perseverance) which would, as I have said, entail salvation by our own works, but it was according to His love and mercy that He chose us for salvation (*Deut.* 7:6, *Rom.* 11:5, *Titus* 3:4–5). The election of God is not a general ordination to eternal life of all who, as God foresees, will turn to him in faith; but it is a personal election, the *fruit* of which is always faith in the Lord Jesus Christ. 'As many as had been appointed to eternal life believed' (*Acts* 13:48). The *reason* for a man's election is simply that it pleased the Lord to have mercy on him; for we read: '(For *the children* not yet being born, nor having done any good or evil, that the purpose God according to election might stand, not of works but of Him who calls), it was said to her [Rebecca], "The older shall serve the younger." As it is written, "Jacob I have loved, but Esau I have hated"' (*Rom.* 9:11–13). It might at this point be objected: Is not God unrighteous to appoint men to salvation in this way? 'Certainly not!', says Paul, 'For He says to Moses, "*I will have mercy on whomever I will have mercy, and I will have compassion on whomever I will have compassion.*" So then *it is* not of him who wills, nor of him who runs, but of God who shows mercy' (*Rom.* 9:14–16). Far from being unrighteous, we have seen that God could righteously condemn every man, woman and child on this earth to eternal damnation, for all have deserved this end. Yet it pleased the Lord to have mercy upon some, to save and deliver some from this dreadful judgement – indeed 'a great multitude, which no one could number' (*Rev.* 7:9). Such is the grace and mercy of our God!

The ground, then, of our salvation is our election. We are saved because it was His will. This absolute election on a personal basis to salvation is something in which the believer ought to rejoice, and for which he ought humbly to thank God, as Jesus did (*Matt.* 11:25), and as Paul did (*2 Thess.* 2:13). 'Rejoice', said the Lord Jesus, 'because your names are written in heaven' (*Luke* 10:20). Here lies our guarantee of salvation – that God Himself chose us from the beginning to be His. His Spirit bears witness with ours that we are the children of God, and because of this we can be sure that on the last day, when the Son sits in judgement and the books are opened, our names will be found written in the Lamb's Book of Life, and He Himself will say to us: 'Come, you blessed of My Father, inherit the kingdom *prepared for you from the foundation of the world*' (*Matt.* 25:34).

Its purpose. It is primarily the glory of God (*Eph.* 1:6,12). But the election of saints is spoken of in Scripture as being but the first act by which God saves those on whom He has set His love. Those God *fore-knew* (that is, knew before as His chosen people; those on whom He had set His love in election to salvation, *1 Pet.* 1:2, *Rom.* 11:2), 'He also predestined *to be* conformed to the image of His Son' and 'whom He predestined, these He also *called*' [by the effectual calling of the Holy Spirit, drawing them to himself]; 'whom He called, these He also *justified*' [by granting to the sinner saving faith in the death of Christ]; 'and whom He justified, these He also *glorified*' (*Rom.* 8:29–30). So the election of saints *ensures* their ultimate salvation as it ensures all the means to that end. Furthermore, Paul writes, 'We are God's workmanship, created in Christ Jesus for good works, which God prepared beforehand that we should walk in them' (*Eph.* 2:10). It also ensures for us the blessedness that comes from knowing that we are at peace with God (*Rom.* 5:1).

The most humbling thing that a Christian can know, and the truth that brings him to his knees before his Lord, is that his salvation is all of grace, that his election was solely of God's will and pleasure. We cannot tell why one dying thief and not the other went with Christ to paradise. We cannot tell why Peter was God's, while Judas was a reprobate. We cannot tell why we should have been born in places where the gospel is preached, while millions never hear it. We can only say that it was the will of God that it should be so, that it was due to His great electing purpose. When we discover truths in Scripture that we find hard from a human standpoint, we should remember that the mystery lies in the will of God, which we can never fathom or know; that we are humbly to accept without reservation what God has revealed to us, not arguing about what He has seen fit not to reveal (*Deut.* 29:29); and, above all, that we should live to the praise of God, in awareness that the purposes of God, not only in the salvation of sinners but in all things, cannot be thwarted but will surely come to pass. 'Oh, the depth of the riches both of the wisdom and knowledge of God! How unsearchable *are* His judgements and His ways past finding out! . . . For of Him and through Him and to Him *are* all things, to whom *be* glory forever. Amen' (*Rom.* 11:33–36).

Questions and Objections Considered

God's election is based on His foreknowledge of who will believe: 'For whom He foreknew, He also predestined . . .' (Rom. 8:29); 'Elect according to the foreknowledge of God the Father' (1 Pet. 1:2).

This objection springs from the mistaken idea that the foreknowledge spoken of in these verses is merely a passive perceiving of what will come to pass. This is certainly the common usage in English; but the concepts of knowledge and foreknowledge in Scripture are far deeper. Let us take some other examples: 'Him [Jesus], being delivered by the determined purpose and foreknowledge of God, you have taken by lawless hands, have crucified, and put to death' (*Acts* 2:23). This foreknowledge is clearly active – almost equivalent to foreordination. 'God has not cast away His people whom He foreknew' (*Rom.* 11:2). Here, as in many other places in the Scriptures, to 'know' is used to express a deep personal relationship of love and choice. See, for example, Matthew 7:23: 'I never knew you; depart from Me, you who practice lawlessness!' Or John 10:14: 'I am the good shepherd; and I know My *sheep*, and am known by my own.' Or Amos 3:2: 'You only have I known of all the families of the earth: Therefore I will punish you for all your iniquities.'

The two verses quoted in the heading are misinterpreted in this way: that God foresees that certain men will of their own free will believe, and He therefore elects them to salvation. This is imposition, rather than exposition! The verses themselves say nothing about foreknowledge of faith or of anything else; nor does any phrase need to be supplied. The foreknowledge here spoken of refers to God's eternal love toward His elect. It carries with it the idea of entering into communion with a view to conferring special favour.

In the Bible, faith is always regarded as the result of election, the gift of God. Never is God's election the ratification of man's choice. 'As many as had been appointed to eternal life believed' (*Acts* 13:48). 'We give thanks to God always for you all . . . knowing, beloved brethren, your election by God. For our gospel did not come to you in word only, but also in power, and in the Holy Spirit and in much assurance' (*1 Thess.* 1:2). 'But we are bound to give thanks to God always for you, brethren beloved by the Lord, because God from the beginning chose you for salvation through sanctification by the Spirit and belief in the truth' (*2 Thess.* 2:13). 'For to you it has been granted on behalf of Christ, not only to believe on Him, but also to suffer for His sake' (*Phil.* 1:29). To Paul, then, and therefore to us also, faith is an evidence of election, and is one of the means ordained by God for the realization of His purposes. Indeed, it was for the salvation of the elect that Paul worked and suffered as he did (*2 Tim.* 2:10).

Careful reading of Ephesians chapter 1 and Romans chapter 9 makes it clear that God's election is absolutely independent of any condition whatever to be fulfilled by us.

God's election is of races and nations, not of individuals.

The argument here is this: the election spoken of in

the Bible is an election of nations. In the Old Testament dispensation God chose Israel to be His people. Moreover when Paul speaks of election in Romans 9, he quotes in verse 13 from Malachi 1:2–3, where the prophet clearly has in view the *nations* of Israel and Edom and not the individuals Jacob and Esau. The whole argument of Romans 9–11 is concerned with God's dealings with Israel as a nation; individuals are not the apostle's immediate concern.

This is what is said, but I hope to show how slender the evidence for this assertion is. I do not deny that God deals with nations. However, even here, we must not forget that nations are composed of individuals. Our holy and just Lord does not raise up or cast down a nation irrespective of those individuals who make up the nation, as if He were to see them as mere statistics.

Although Scripture does speak of national election, in the vast majority of cases it is the election of *individuals* which is in view. Consider Matthew 24:24, John 6:65, John 15:6; Romans 8:28–30 and 33, 1 Corinthians 1:26–31, Ephesians 1:3–5 and 11–12; 1 Thessalonians 1:4–5, 2 Thessalonians 1:13, 2 Timothy 2:10, Titus 1:1, 1 Peter 1:2 and 2 Peter 1:10. The reader who has looked up even some of these verses will need no further demonstration that God chooses individuals for salvation.

Yet this objection ought not to be left without a consideration of Paul's argument in Romans 9, for it is in this chapter that we see most clearly God's absolute sovereignty in election, and it would be damaging (though by no means fatal) to the gospel of grace if it were to be shown that the election here spoken of is not of individuals, but of nations. Here is an outline of Romans, chapters 1-11, with particular detail in chapters 9-11.

Introduction (1:1–15)
Theme: The gospel (1:16–17)
The sin of man and the judgement of God (1:18–32)
Jews and Gentiles alike guilty before God (2:1–3:20)
Justification by faith alone (3:21–4:25)
Righteousness and life in Christ (5:1–21)
Living under grace (6:1–23)
The law and sin in the Christian life (7:1–25)
Living by the Holy Spirit (8:1–27)
The eternal security of the elect (8:28–39)

Objection: God's purposes for Israel seem to have failed, for they, the chosen people, have been cast off through unbelief (9:1–5)

Answer: God's Word has *not* failed (9:6):
Not all the natural children of Abraham are entitled to the promise:

     Example 1: Isaac, not Ishmael (9:7–9)
     Example 2: Jacob, not Esau (9:10–13)

God is not unrighteous, for His actions are sovereign (9:14–18)
No-one is entitled to question God's actions (9:19–21)
God demonstrates His power, wrath and mercy (9:22–23)
He has saved many of the Gentiles, and a remnant of Israel (9:24–30)

Explanation of Israel's unbelief: a contrast between justification by faith and by works of the law (9:31–10:5)
The free offer to all of salvation through faith (10:6–13)
The necessity of preaching the gospel (10:14–21)

God has *not* cast Israel away, because:
> (1) There is a *remnant* according to the election of grace, though the rest have been blinded (11:1–10)
> (2) Israel's fall is not final. If their fall brought salvation to the Gentiles, how much more will their inclusion (11:11–15)! Warning of the impartiality of God (11:16–22)
> (3) Israel shall be saved in the future (11:23–32)

Doxology: The unsearchable counsels and all-sufficiency of God (11:33–36)

Bearing this outline in mind, we see that Paul answers the charge against God that His promises to Israel have failed by showing that in fact the promises were made to the nation as comprising elect *individuals*, for example Isaac and Jacob, and so the promises have been fulfilled to the elect remnant. Both the objections and Paul's replies in chapter 9:14–23 lose all their force if the discussion at this point is about nations. The fact that Paul quotes Malachi is no valid objection to this, for the prophet emphasizes that God deals with the two nations according to His purposes for their individual parents. Luther's *Bondage of the Will* is recommended reading for all who are concerned to look into this question further.

God has stated that He has 'no pleasure in the death of the wicked, but that the wicked turn from his way and live' (Ezek. 33:11), and that He is 'not willing that any should perish but that all should come to repentance' (2 Pet. 3:9).

The verse in 2 Peter is variously interpreted by commentators. Some believe from the context ('longsuffering toward us') that it is the elect and God's purpose to save all of them which is spoken of; others believe that the verse speaks of God's general desire that all men should repent, as in Ezekiel 33:11.

If we adopt the more general interpretation, both verses teach much the same thing. God does not condemn the wicked gladly. He takes no pleasure in the pains of hell. Rather, He is pleased when any sinner repents. Sinners who are finally lost are those who refuse to repent, and God manifests His holiness and justice in their punishment.

Why then, it is asked, does not God elect all to salvation? We reply, why should He save any? Despite His goodness, men of their own accord universally refuse to repent. It is a mark of God's great mercy that He chooses to save some. No man has any right to question God's actions, as if we could judge the Lord of glory. We ought not to forget that God's purposes are not decided only by His mercy, but by His wisdom, in which He displays also His justice and power.

A right balance between God's sovereignty and man's responsibility is this: When a soul is lost, the fault is entirely its own; when a soul is saved, the glory is entirely God's.

As God's promises in the gospel are universal, if He is sincere the possibility of salvation cannot be restricted to a pre-chosen few. The Bible says, 'Whoever calls on the name of the Lord shall be saved' (Rom. 10:13).

It is indeed a mystery which we cannot understand that God sincerely offers the gospel of salvation freely to all, while He has purposed to save only those whom He has chosen. Yet we are to believe it, for Scripture teaches both. Here is one of the paradoxes of the Word of God which our feeble minds cannot resolve but which our hearts receive by faith.

Yet it may be worth commenting that the sincerity of a promise is proved by its fulfilment. And the glorious fact is that these promises of God have in every single instance been found true.

Everyone without exception who has called on the name of the Lord *has* been saved. Not one who has trusted in Christ has perished. There has never been a person who has *wanted* to come to Christ, who has found God's decree of election to be a barrier in the way.

The promises are universal in that no-one is excluded. But they are for those who come and take them. There are no gracious promises for those who *will not* believe. That is why we must beseech men to believe in Christ, so that they make take to themselves God's promises; and we know that they are enabled to do so as the Lord quickens their dead hearts and removes their unwillingness and stubbornness.

God cannot be just if He elects some to be saved, while others are passed over to be left to the consequences of their sins, which is eternal damnation.

If God is to be charged with dealing unjustly with men, it will have to be shown that men in some way *deserve* what God has been pleased to bestow upon some, and to deny to others – the eternal salvation of their souls. We have seen, however, that all men *deserve* only Satan's wages, which are eternal death and hell. God could, accordingly, be perfectly just in condemning all men to damnation. The Christian marvels, therefore, that, in contrast to the blackness of despair which he felt when it was shown to him that by the law of God he stood condemned and must inevitably hear the dreadful words 'Depart from me, you cursed, into the eternal fire', another message shines out from God's Word: The Lord is 'gracious and merciful, slow to anger, and of great kindness' (*Joel* 2:13), and in this is his hope. If a man is saved, it is because of God's mercy and grace – God's free and *unmerited* favour towards sinners; if a man is condemned, he is *justly* condemned for his own sins. Romans 6:23 is a universally loved verse, because it contrasts what the sinner deserves with what he receives as a free gift from God. However, it is the prerogative of the Giver to distribute the gift as He will (*Rom.* 9:15), and the justice of God would remain unimpaired whether God had chosen not to save anybody, or to save all men.

The decrees of God, let it not be forgotten, are secret decrees, 'For who has known the mind of the Lord?' (*Rom.* 11:34). The mortal who dares question the counsels of the Most High and blame God for injustice is swiftly silenced by Paul: 'O man, who are you to reply against God? Will the thing formed say to him who formed *it*, "Why have you made me like this?" Does not the potter have power over the clay, from the same lump to make one vessel for honour and another for dishonour?' (*Rom.* 9:20–21).

The Christian is not the possessor of a salvation to which he has any right, but a debtor to the mercy of an all-wise and just God.

If the salvation of individuals depends on God's decree of election, then there is no motive for evangelism, since all whom God purposes to save will certainly be saved.

If for no other reason, the preaching of the gospel is justified, at the most basic level, by the express command of the Lord Jesus Christ (*Matt.* 28:19) and by the example and exhortations of the apostles. It was said by D. L. Moody: 'One plain text is as good as a thousand reasons.' God's counsels are secret; we do not know who is or who is not elect, except by observing signs of true regeneration – 'You will know them by their fruits' – amongst which are repentance and faith in the Lord Jesus Christ. The God-appointed means by which man comes to faith is the preaching of the gospel (*Rom.* 10:14); and this, surely, is the proper answer to such an objection.

Furthermore, far from being a barrier to evangelism, the doctrine of election is the one thing that makes evangelism worthwhile. In fact, it actually gives us our only hope of success, because it gives us the certainty that our evangelism will be fruitful! We can evangelize in the sure knowledge that God in His grace has chosen a great multitude from every tribe and tongue and nation whom He will definitely save. This is what gave the Apostle Paul the greatest confidence as he preached the gospel throughout the Mediterranean world. When, for example, he was having a hard time in Corinth, the Lord spoke to him one night in a vision, 'Do not be afraid, but speak, and do not keep silent . . . I have many people in this city' (*Acts* 18:9–10). Through the preaching of the gospel, God's elect will be saved and God's cause will ultimately triumph for His honour and glory. On the other hand, God is not glorified by the Christian looking for the softest pillow he can find while the eternal purposes are being worked out. This is the position of the so-called hyper-Calvinists. It seems hardly necessary to say that their views are quite unscriptural and false.

Jesus said, 'All authority has been given to Me in heaven and on earth. Go therefore and make disciples of all the nations.' He commands us to be faithful in sowing. God promises that of the seed sown some will spring up to eternal life. The weeping of sowing will be turned into the rejoicing of reaping as the roll of God's elect is filled up and those whose names were from eternity written in the Book of Life find their salvation in Christ.

God loves all alike; hence there cannot be an unconditional decree of election to salvation.

We must be clear about what we mean when we say that God loves all men alike. There are two senses to

[57]

be given to the word 'loves' in this context; in one sense, God does indeed love all men; in the other, the Scriptures assert that He does not.

The distinction to be drawn is between God's love for men as their Creator, and His love for men as their Redeemer. Inasmuch as God has created all men and has pronounced His creation good, although now marred by sin, it can truly be said that God 'hates nothing that He has made'. He demonstrates this love as Creator by His providential care for His creatures. In this sense, God is the 'Saviour of all men' (*1 Tim*. 4:10). We must not lose sight of this important truth of the *universal* love of God, which we have mentioned in Chapter 1.

However, the Scriptures plainly teach that God's love as Redeemer is a *particular* love, manifested toward those upon whom He has set his love in their election, redemption, calling and glorification. It is a love from which nothing can separate God's own: 'For I am persuaded that neither death nor life . . . nor any other created thing, shall be able to separate us from the love of God which is in Christ Jesus our Lord' (*Rom*. 8:38–39). That God's redemptive love does not extend to all men is plainly taught in Malachi 1:2–3, this passage being cited by Paul in Romans 9:11–13: '(For *the children* not yet being born, nor having done any good or evil, that the purpose God according to election might stand, not of works but of Him who calls), it was said to her [Rebecca], "The older shall serve the younger." As it is written, "Jacob I have loved, but Esau I have hated".'

The whole truth lies not at either the Arminian nor the Calvinistic extreme, but at both extremes together.

The objection that the truth about the doctrines of the gospel is a balance between 'Calvinism' and 'Arminianism' is a common one, stemming generally from a praiseworthy desire to arrive at the true scriptural balance between the doctrines emphasizing, on the one hand, the sovereignty of God, and on the other hand, the responsibility of man. The objection is frequently supported by appeals to the teaching of Charles Simeon:

Sometimes I am a high Calvinist, at other times a low Arminian, so that if extremes will please you, I am your man; only remember, it is not *one* extreme we are to go to, but *both* extremes.

and to the notion that the differences between Wesley and Whitefield resulted from the possession by each of but 'one half of the truth' concerning the doctrines of grace. The objection, then, is that the Calvinistic account of the matter, which we have put forward in this book, is one-sided; it is not that the account, in its positive aspects, is *wrong*, but that on its own it does not faithfully reflect the balance of Scripture, which, it is said, teaches the free will of man as well as the sovereign election of God. Applications of this idea are often succinctly expressed: that one should be 'a Calvinist on one's knees, and an Arminian on one's feet'; that one should 'pray as if it all depended upon God, and work as if it all depended upon oneself'.

In answering this objection, I shall consider first the absurdities to which it inevitably leads, and second those parts of Scripture from which it claims to draw support.

First then, the absurdities in which this teaching involves its adherents. If we follow it consistently, we must, on our knees, thank God for His eternal election, while on our feet we inform sinners that salvation in fact rests upon their exercise of free-will. In other words, what we say before God must be contradicted by what we say before the world. That this should be the consequence of such opinions is hardly surprising, since, as I have endeavoured to show, Calvinism and Arminianism, far from being complementary, are irreconcilably opposed to each other. To assert the one doctrine is to deny, implicitly and explicitly, the other; and the claim that such contradictory 'truths' are to be found side by side in Holy Scripture, which is the Word of the God who cannot lie, must therefore be a claim that rests upon faulty exegesis of the text.

Secondly, let us look at some Scriptures which are often taken to show that 'Calvinistic' and 'Arminian' doctrines are taught side by side. It will be seen that, in all such cases, the true paradox is not that between sovereignty and free will, which would indeed lead to the Calvinist-Arminian antithesis, but that between sovereignty and responsibility. I would refer at this point to the previous discussion on the difference between free will and responsibility in Chapter 1.

Often quoted in this context is John 6:37. The first part of the verse speaks of the electing and predestinating purposes of the Father in giving a people to the Son, while the second part of the verse, as some claim, teaches that those who will not ultimately be cast out are those who have come to Christ as a result of their own free will.

It may readily be seen, however, that this interpretation is seriously at fault. No-one can come to the Lord Jesus Christ of his own ability, for his nature is sinful and his will is depraved. All, therefore, who do come to Christ, come because they have been given to Him by the Father. That they come willingly shows that their minds have begun to be illuminated by the Holy Spirit.

Those who thus come will never be cast out, because the calling of God is *effectual*, that is, God's purposes are *realized*. And the realization of God's purpose in the giving spoken of in the first part of the verse is the union of His elect with Christ, which is precisely what is expressed by the words 'will by no means cast out'.

The two-edged truth of sovereignty and responsibility is taught with clarity in Matthew 11:25–30. Here again, it is wrong exegesis to turn the gracious invitation of the Lord Jesus into a proof-text for free will, and hence into an 'Arminian verse'. The invitation makes it clear that casting the burden on to the Lord Jesus Christ is a *responsible* action; but the inference, 'responsibility, therefore free will' is, as I have shown previously, purely philosophical, resting upon nothing in Scripture. Those who oppose the doctrines which have been put forward with the charge that 'Calvinists are being more logical than Scripture' appear not to have noticed the beam that is in their own eye. The balance of Scripture, let it be said once again, is the balance between the sovereignty of God and the responsibility of man, and these are truths which have always been taught by those known as Calvinists.

Whenever God acts within man's terms of reference there are bound to be paradoxical mysteries which we, possessing only finite minds and intelligence, are unable to comprehend. For example, the man with the withered hand mentioned in the gospel (*Mark* 3:1–5) stretched forth his hand. It was most certainly he who did it; but the man's entire enabling was from the Lord Jesus Christ and Him alone.

Whenever Christ spoke the word of enablement, no sufferer mentioned in the gospels could ever plead inability to obey the command. In the epistles we find Paul writing: 'To this *end* I also labour, striving according to His workng which works in me mightily' (*Col.* 1:29), and again, 'But by the grace of God I am what I am, and His grace toward me was not in vain; but I laboured more abundantly than they all, yet not I, but the grace of God *which was* with me' (*1 Cor.* 15:10). Here are classic statements of God's sovereignty and man's responsibility.

But to equate the doctrines of sovereignty with 'the Calvinistic truth' and the doctrines of responsibility with 'the Arminian truth' is to have misunderstood what Calvinism really is. The Calvinist is not embarrassed by those parts of Scripture which emphasize the responsibility of man, nor does he presume to recommend to the inspired writers that they alter some of their expressions that seem a little 'broad'. The Calvinist rejoices in the free offer of the gospel to all men; for what preachers were more fond of pressing home to their hearers the responsibilities of the gospel than the Calvinistic Puritans and their successors?

I repeat that it is hyper-Calvinism, and not Calvinism, that emphasizes the sovereignty of God at the expense of the responsibility of man. If, then, we are convinced of the truth of the doctrines popularly styled 'Calvinistic', let us be wholehearted in preaching the gospel with the courage of our convictions.

It is perhaps advisable to add that the use of the label 'Calvinism' does not imply that we believe these things because Calvin said them. John Newton commented on this misapprehension in a letter to a friend:

> I remember that, three or four years ago, I mentioned some part of the gospel truth to a gentleman who called on me here, and he answered, 'If it is a truth, you are indebted for it to Calvin.' As well might he have said, because Calvin had seen the sun, and has mentioned it in his writings, we build our knowledge of its light and influence upon his testimony. These are acknowledged throughout the world, whenever there is an eye to behold them. Here the courtier and the clown, the philosopher and the savage, are upon a level.

If the doctrine of election is true, then it follows that all those who are not elect are infallibly predestined to condemnation, come what may. The author of such a decree cannot be the God of mercy and love revealed in the Bible.

The first thing to be said in connection with the doctrine of reprobation here being spoken of is that the Scriptures tell us much more about God's decrees and purposes with regard to those being saved than with regard to those who perish. The gospel is good news, proclaiming to lost sinners an incomparable Saviour who delivers from the wrath to come. But since one of the principal objections to the doctrine of election is that it necessarily entails reprobation, it is important that the scriptural teaching on the subject should be examined.

It is, as the objector rightly points out, a truth of logic that if God has purposed to save some, then He has also purposed not to save others. But not only is it a logical truth: it is also a scriptural one. The Lord Jesus Christ thanked His Father that He had 'hidden these things from the wise and prudent' (*Matt.* 11:25). Paul declares that God 'has mercy on whom He wills, and whom He wills He hardens', for, 'Does not the potter have power over the clay, from the same lump to make one vessel for honour and another for dishonour?' (*Rom.* 9:18, 21). Peter speaks of those who are 'disobedient to the word, to which they also were appointed' (*1 Pet.* 2:8), while Jude warns his readers of 'certain men' who 'long ago were marked out for this condemnation' (*Jude* 4). It is clear, then, from Scripture, that God has decreed, or purposed, to do from eternity what He actually does in time in regard to those who perish, as well as in regard to those who are saved.

The doctrine of reprobation may be stated thus: 'The rest of mankind God was pleased . . . to pass by; and to ordain them to dishonour and wrath for their sin' (*Westminster Confession* iii, 7). It includes two distinct acts: that of *passing by,* which is simply 'decreeing to leave – and in consequence leaving – men in their natural state of sin, to withhold from them, or to abstain from conferring upon them, those special, supernatural, gracious influences, which are necessary to enable them to repent and believe', the result of which is that they continue in their sin and guilt; and that of *foreordination to damnation,* which is a judicial act by which God ordains such men to condemnation *on account of their sin.* It is very important to note that the punishment to which God has foreordained the non-elect is a *deserved* punishment. It is God's justice which requires that their sin be punished. The decree is founded upon, and has reference to, their sin as a thing certain and contemplated. So it is that God is just, for the condemnation of a sinner is due to his own sin. There is little in Scripture to suggest that God's decrees of election and reprobation contemplate men other than as in their fallen and sinful state, so that the sovereign act of reprobation is a simple decree *not* to save, rather than a positive decree to damn a certain number arbitrarily (which would mean that men were *made* sinners to fit them for destruction).

[65]

The grace of God shines all the more brightly when we consider that, because all have sinned, all could justly have been passed by. Furthermore, it is worth noting that, while an elect and justified sinner can receive assurance from the Holy Spirit of his eternal salvation, and it is indeed God's will that he should, it is not the case that anyone can *know* himself to be foreordained to eternal damnation. Unregenerate men, in general, do not care; whereas the troubles of those that do are generally evidence of a work of grace of the Holy Spirit or of conviction prior to regeneration. While there is life, there is indeed hope; the offer of the gospel is held out to all, and God's grace can rescue the most wretched of sinners.

In conclusion, it is worth recalling some words of William Cunningham:

> Calvinists do not shrink from discussing the subject of reprobation, though, from its awful character, they have no satisfaction in dwelling upon it, and feel deeply the propriety of being peculiarly careful here not to attempt to be wise above what is written . . . There is something about God's decrees and purposes, even in regard to those who perish, which can be resolved only into His own good pleasure, into the most wise and holy counsel of His will.

The doctrine of election eliminates assurance.

The argument here is that, because of God's decree of election, the believer can, on this earth, have no assurance of eternal salvation, since he must always be asking himself whether he is elect or reprobate.

But, in fact, the exact opposite is the case! For the Christian, whose soul has been set free by the Son, with whose spirit the Holy Spirit bears witness that he is a child of God (*Rom.* 8:16), the grand reason, and the only reason, for his assurance is that his salvation is entirely a work of grace, purposed by God from before the foundation of the world. He begins to realize that the good work begun in him God will assuredly bring to completion at the day of Jesus Christ, and, with the knowledge that he is predestined to a glorious eternity in the presence of Him who loved his soul, he is able with assurance to say:

> *Yes, I to the end shall endure,*
> *As sure as the earnest is given.*

Article xvii of the Church of England says:

> . . . The godly consideration of predestination, and our election in Christ, is full of sweet, pleasant and unspeakable comfort to godly persons, and such as feel in themselves the working of the Spirit of Christ, mortifying the works of the flesh, and their earthly members, and drawing up their mind to high and heavenly things, as well because it doth greatly establish and confirm their faith of eternal salvation to be enjoyed through Christ, as because it doth fervently kindle their love towards God . . .

Before leaving the subject, however, a protest should be registered against the shallow teaching on assurance that is current amongst many evangelicals.

Frequently the first thing that the young convert is told is: 'If you have taken the step and made a decision for Christ, then you are definitely a Christian. To doubt that you are a Christian is to doubt the Word of God.'

The effect of such teaching is very dangerous and a perversion of the Bible. Sinners are told, on the basis of their decision for Christ, that they have eternal life, even if they have experienced no conviction of sin and have not been brought to an end of their confidence in themselves. They do not expect to become changed people because they have never been taught that when God's Spirit performs a work of grace the result is a *new* creation. They do not look for evidences, in terms of spiritual fruit, of their regeneration, by which the Christian's calling and election are made sure, because they have been told that once they have made their decision, no matter what they do subsequently, they have been saved.

Yet true God-given assurance is always accompanied by an awareness of sin being mortified. It is Scripture that commands us to examine our lives and to test ourselves to see if we are in the faith. It is to be feared that because many have cried, 'Peace, peace; when there is no peace' with God – because there is no true work of grace in the heart – there are people in our evangelical churches who sincerely believe themselves to be saved because they cry 'Lord, Lord', even though they do not do the things which the Lord says.

To such people He will one day pronounce those dreadful words: 'Depart from me, you evil doers.'

'Let him who thinks he stands take heed lest he falls' (*1 Cor.* 10:12).

A final comment on the privilege of true assurance from Thomas Brooks:

> The being in a state of grace makes a man's condition happy, safe, and sure; but the seeing, the knowing of himself to be in such a state, is that which renders his life sweet and comfortable. The being in a state of grace will yield a man a heaven hereafter, but the seeing of himself in this state will yield him both a heaven here and a heaven hereafter; it will render him doubly blessed, blest in heaven, and blessed in his own conscience (*Heaven on Earth*, Banner of Truth Trust edition, p. 14).

4

Salvation Accomplished

A ccording to the divine plan of salvation, that is to say, 'the mystery which has been hidden from ages and from generations, but has now been revealed to His saints' (*Col.* 1:26), our salvation is a work of the triune God, Father, Son and Holy Spirit; the Father in election; the Son in redemption; and the Spirit in regeneration and sanctification. 'A plan', says Charles Hodge, 'supposes: (1) the selection of some definite end or object to be accomplished; (2) the choice of appropriate means; (3) at least in the case of God, the effectual application and control of those means to the accomplishment of the contemplated end.' In this plan of salvation, the end, to which the death of the Lord Jesus Christ was the means, was the reconciliation with God of His people, through their redemption; and this redemption and reconciliation were infallibly secured at the cross of Calvary. Here it was that in His plan to save those on whom He had been pleased to have mercy, God's elect were redeemed from sin and their eternal salvation made certain.

The *purpose* of Christ's coming is clearly stated in Scripture. He came 'to seek and to save that which was lost'; He came 'into the world to save sinners'; He came 'to give His life a ransom for many' (*Luke* 19:1, *1 Tim.* 1:15, *Matt.* 20:28), that whoever lives and believes in Him should never die (*John* 11:26); for these, who would later believe in Him, Christ gave Himself, to 'deliver us from this present evil age, according to the will of our God and Father' (*Gal.* 1:4). These, for whom He died, constitute His church: He 'loved the church and gave Himself for her, that He might sanctify and cleanse her with the washing of water by the word, that He might present her to Himself a glorious church, not having spot or wrinkle or any such thing, but that she should be holy and without blemish' (*Eph.* 5:25–27). As John Owen says, 'These last words express also the very aim and end of Christ in giving himself for any, even that they might be made *fit* for God, and brought nigh unto him.' So we read in Titus 2:14: 'Who gave Himself for us, that He might redeem us from every lawless deed and purify for Himself *His* own special people, zealous for good works.' In other words, all whom the Father had given to Christ (*John* 10:29), those whom God had chosen for Himself, the elect, Jesus Christ undertook to redeem from the curse of the law by becoming a curse for them (*Gal.* 3:13), enduring for them the judgement of God which was their just due.

I am aware that the question 'For whom did Christ die?' is a controversial one; yet I hold that the atonement described in Scripture is *particular* – the Lord

Jesus Christ died specifically for the elect, as their representative and substitute, to secure their salvation. As Christ came into the world to *save* sinners, so I hold that the cross makes certain the salvation of all those for whom Christ died. To hold that He died for all men leads either to the conclusion that all men are thereby saved (which Scripture denies), or that His death only made salvation possible for all, and not certain for any (which Scripture also denies), or that His death was not truly substitutionary at all (whereas Scripture plainly says that it was). I shall consider these points later; for the moment, I want to establish the truth that Christ died for His church, and not for the sins of each and every individual.

Firstly, particular atonement alone makes sense of the particular love of God the Father and the particular calling and regeneration of the Holy Spirit. I have already emphasized that God is sovereign in salvation. This means that He is its Author, and that He grants it to whom He pleases, to those of His own choice. God's election is particular. For His own glory He had mercy upon whom He would, and He passed by the rest, leaving them to their just condemnation. The Holy Spirit's calling is particular: He works in the hearts of those whom God has loved, bringing them to new birth, granting them repentance and faith, and obedience to the Word of God. So too, then, the atoning work of the one Mediator between God and man is particular: He died for God's elect that they might be justified. 'He who did not spare His own Son, but delivered Him up for us all, how shall He not with Him also freely give us all things? Who shall bring a charge against God's elect? *It is* God who justifies. Who *is* He who condemns? *It is* Christ who died, and furthermore is also risen, who is even at the right hand of God, who also makes intercession for us' (*Rom.* 8:32–34).

Secondly, the will of God is always accomplished. What He is pleased to purpose will surely come to pass. So, as it was the purpose of Christ's coming to save sinners, that is exactly what was achieved; and, by the cross, sinners are saved by being washed in the blood of Christ which was shed for them.

> *There is a fountain filled with blood,*
> *Drawn from Immanuel's veins;*
> *And sinners, plunged beneath that flood,*
> *Lose all their guilty stains.*

No one who believes the teaching of Christ concerning the condemnation of unbelievers would deny that the benefits of Christ's death – redemption from sin, reconciliation with God, forgiveness – are enjoyed only by those who believe; for only these are reconciled to God (*Rom.* 5:10, *Eph.* 2:16), justified in His sight and sanctified (*Heb.* 9:14; 13:12, *1 John* 1:7, *Eph.* 5:25–27), and adopted into His family (*Gal.* 4:4–5, *Rom.* 8:15). But since these things were achieved at the cross, and appropriated by a certain group of people (who believe), I maintain that they were intended for those by whom they are possessed (the elect). Otherwise the purposes of God in sending His Son become no more than pious hopes and vain wishes for the salvation of the world, for all mankind. The Bible sets forth a redemption that is *personal.* 'The Son of God loved me, and gave Himself for me' (*Gal.* 2:20) is the testimony of every born-again soul, because Jesus died that that soul might live.

Thirdly, the church is the bride of Christ (*Rev.* 21: 2), which He loves with an everlasting love. Here again, we see the forcefulness and deep meaning of the metaphor of marriage. The essence of the bride-bridegroom relationship is that the groom knows and loves the bride; so, when the Lord Jesus loved the church and gave Himself for her, He was giving Himself for a bride whom He already *knew* and cared for (*Jer.* 31:3, *Eph.* 5:25, *Song of Sol.* 2:2). By His death, He delivered His bride from darkness and brought her into the banqueting-house, the place of rejoicing, where the union takes place (*Song of Sol.* 2:4, *Col.* 1:13, *Matt.* 25:10). If Christ died for all men, then He has a bride whom He does not know and therefore cannot love with the particular love that every bridegroom has for his spouse.

Fourthly, God is just. All sin must be punished, but He does not require it to be punished twice over. The Lord Jesus Christ died as our representative, inasmuch as those for whom He died were themselves condemned, in His person, at the cross. When He died, they died in Him, and in His resurrection they passed from death to life (*2 Cor.* 5:14–17). To all those who died, in Christ, on the cross, there is no more condemnation (*Rom.* 8:1) because they have already been condemned; their Substitute 'became sin' for them. God cannot, therefore, condemn a man for whom Christ died, since Christ paid the penalty for his sin once and for all. But since those (like Judas) who are condemned are not saved, Christ cannot have died for them, for God does not demand two payments for the same sin. Under the New Covenant, Christ's blood was accepted as a full, perfect and sufficient sacrifice for that sin. If any one man perishes for whom Christ died, then God is unjust indeed. Jesus came to *save* sinners, and that is exactly what He does, by His death.

> *The terrors of law and of God*
> *With me can have nothing to do;*
> *My Saviour's obedience and blood*
> *Hide all my transgressions from view.*

It is my contention that this doctrine of particular, or, as it is often misleadingly termed, 'limited' atonement, alone does justice to the free saving grace of God, and is the only atonement to be found in His Word. If we say that Christ died for all men, then we must also say that Christ died that any man might live if . . . and then follow certain conditions of salvation. Yet, the grace of God is freely (*Rom.* 3:24; 6:23) and unconditionally given to helpless sinners. Christ's death ensured the calling and keeping – the present and final salvation – of all whose sins He bore. That is what Calvary meant, and means. The cross *saved*; the cross *saves*.

This, the saving power of the blood of the Lamb, is why the cross stands at the very centre of the Christian faith.

Questions and Objections Considered

There are many verses which declare that Christ died for the world, or for all men.

It is true that Scripture says that Christ died for the world (*John* 1:29; 3:16; 4:42; 6:51, *2 Cor.* 5:19, *1 John* 2:2; 4:14). It also says that He died for all (*Isa.* 53:6, *John* 12:32, *2 Cor.* 5:14–15, *1 Tim.* 2:6, *Heb.* 2:9) though it is noteworthy that the expression 'all men' is found only once in connection with the death of Christ (*Rom.* 5:18). In all other cases where it is found in English versions, the word 'men' has been supplied by the translators.

It might seem that these texts prove the case for universal redemption. But this is to take a superficial view of the question. In fact, these verses may be legitimately understood in such a way as to agree with the biblical evidence already adduced for particular redemption. There are three lines of argument which I shall discuss: first, that the terms 'world' and 'all', though universal in form, are very frequently used in Scripture with limited or indefinite reference; second, that a more detailed exegesis of these verses in context shows that universalism is not intended; and third, that a universalistic interpretation contradicts the scriptural witness to the nature of Christ's death.

The meanings of the word 'world' in Scripture are briefly as follows:

1. The habitable earth, or, more generally, the created universe (*Job* 34:13, *Psa.* 24:1; 90:2, *Matt.* 13:38; 26:13, *Acts* 17:24, *Eph.* 1:4; *1 Tim.* 1:15).

2. The inhabitants of the earth.
   (i) Each and every individual (*Rom.* 3:6, 19).
   (ii) Men in general, or many (*Matt.* 24:14, *Luke* 2:1, *John* 7:4; 12:19; 16:8; 17:21, *Rom.* 1:8; 10:18, *1 Cor.* 4:9, *Col.* 1:6).

3. Evil.
   (i) Wicked men, as opposed to God's people (*Isa.* 13:11, *John* 7:7; 14:17, 22; 15:19; 17:9, 25, *1 Cor.* 6:2; 11:32, *Heb.* 11:38, *1 John* 5:19, *Rev.* 13:3).

   (ii) Men generally, in their corrupted condition (*Matt.* 18:7, *John* 14:30; 18:36, *Rom.* 12:2, *1 Cor.* 2:12; 7:31, 33, *Gal.* 1:4, *Eph.* 2:2; 6:12, *Col.* 2:8, *James* 1:27, *1 John* 2:15–17; 4:5).

The word 'all' also has different meanings:

1. All of all sorts (*Luke* 24:25, *Acts* 10:36; 20:27, *Rom.* 5:18a, *1 Cor.* 7:17).
2. All of some sorts (*Luke* 4:13, *Rom.* 5:18b, *1 Cor.* 8:1; 15:22, *Eph.* 4:6).
3. Some of all sorts (*Matt.* 9:35, *Mark* 11:32, *Luke* 11:42; 18:12, *Acts* 2:17, *Rom.* 14:2, *1 Cor.* 1:5, *1 Tim.* 2:1–3, 8).

When Christ is said to have died for 'the world' or for 'all', those who wish to demonstrate universal redemption must prove that 'world' is used in sense 2(i), and 'all' in sense 1. It is plain that this is by no means evident on the grounds of usage. The question is not, 'What is the ordinary sense of "world" or "all" in English?' (for the Bible was not written in English); but rather, 'What is the meaning of the word in a particular verse?', and this can only be discovered by studying how that word is used elsewhere in Scripture and in its context.

Having demonstrated that the verses under consideration need not assert universal redemption, I now turn to the second line of argument: exegesis of these verses in context. Lack of space means that only a few of the more important examples can be considered here.

John 3:16: 'For God so loved the world that He gave His only begotten Son, that whoever believes in Him should not perish but have everlasting life.' The purpose of this so-well-known verse is to declare the greatness of the love of God. At once we see the inadequacy of the view that 'the world' means each and every man, for then our attention is concentrated on the vast number of individuals who compose the world; but, great as this is by earthly standards, it is not adequate to measure the love of God. Moreover, on this view, what has God's love done for the 'world'? It has only opened a way of salvation before it, whereas the very next verse asserts that God's purpose is far greater than that – it is actually to *save* the world. Are we to say, then, that 'the world' here means, in effect, 'the elect'? Although this view has much to commend it, it hardly seems to do justice to the concept of 'the world'. And, when we see also that the term is comprehensive, that the world is envisaged as a whole, it seems that we ought to understand 'world' in its primarily *moral* sense: it is that corrupt society of humanity which is under Satan's power and at enmity with God. That this sense (3(ii) in the table given above) is the one most appropriate here is confirmed by the fact that the world is viewed as perishing; and so, although Christ could have come to judge the world, He came rather to save the world. The greatness of God's love is measured by this: that He loves the corrupt and sinful world so much that He sent not judgement but salvation. So by 'the world' here is meant humanity, not quantitatively, but qualitatively. If one insists on asking whether all men are intended, we must reply that they are not, for God's love is here set forth as of saving effect; yet the objects of His love are described not as the elect, but as sinners – to emphasize the mercy and grace of God.

1 John 2:1–2: 'And if any one sins, we have an Advocate with the Father, Jesus Christ the righteous. And He Himself is the propitiation for our sins; and not for ours only, but also for the whole world.' It must certainly be admitted that these verses are quite consistent with universal atonement and that, if that were the overall teaching of Scripture, no more would need to be said. But it is also plain that this statement of the apostle John may be understood in harmony with limited atonement and that, within the scope of his argument, there are several reasons why he should have used the expression 'the whole world' without implying at all that Christ's propitiation extends to the sins of each individual man, any more than His advocacy does. John here contemplates the glory of the work of Christ who is not only the means of propitiation, but is Himself the actual embodiment of propitiation; and so he proclaims Him, with praise and wonder, in *three ways* the propitiation 'for our sins; and not for ours only, but also for the whole world'. First, Christ's propitiation is universal in its *extent* – effective not just for the Jews, or for the believers to whom John writes, but for all in every nation the world over who come into saving union with Him. Secondly, Christ is the *only* propitiation for sin: 'There is no other name under heaven given among men by which we must be saved' (*Acts* 4:12). And thirdly, Christ's propitiation endures *for ever*, always effective 'if anyone sins', and powerful for believers of every age. This is sufficient reason for the expression 'also for the whole world'.

Hebrews 2:9: 'But we see Jesus, who was made a little lower than the angels, for the suffering of death crowned with glory and honour, that He, by the grace of God, might taste death for everyone.' Are we to take 'everyone' to refer to all without exception? Let the context decide. The writer is speaking of the 'many sons' being brought 'to glory'; of 'those who are made holy'; of Christ's 'brethren'; of 'the children whom God has given (Him)' (verses 10–13). There is no reason to extend the reference of verse 9 beyond that of the subsequent verses.

I conclude my discussion and re-emphasize my previous points by a third line of argument: that the nature of Christ's death as described in Scripture, even in the very verses under consideration, is such as to rule out a universalistic view of the atonement. Did Christ die to make men saveable, or to save them? Has He 'obtained eternal redemption' (*Heb.*

9:12) or has He made all men redeemable? The saving power and effectiveness which the concepts of salvation, redemption and propitiation imply cannot be watered down. If Christ has given Himself a ransom for every individual, then every individual must be saved; for God cannot require the ransom payment twice – from Christ and from the sinner also. Since it is apparent from Scripture that not all are saved, and it is equally apparent that the atonement is effective, a universalistic view, though initially plausible from these few verses, just does not hold water.

Limited atonement limits the grace of God.
I have referred to this doctrine as 'Particular Atonement' and not by its more common name of 'Limited Atonement', in order to avoid giving the wrong impression. But of course the objection is not answered by changing the name of the doctrine! I am content to say with C. H. Spurgeon:

> We are often told that we limit the atonement of Christ, because we say that Christ has not made a satisfaction for all men, or all men would be saved. Now, our reply to this is, that, on the other hand, our opponents limit it: we do not. The Arminians say, Christ died for all men. Ask them what they mean by it. Did Christ die so as to secure the salvation of all men? They say, 'No, certainly not.' We ask them the next question – Did Christ die so as to secure the salvation of any man in particular. They answer 'No'. They are obliged to admit this, if they are consistent. They say 'No, Christ has died that any man may be saved if' – and then follow certain conditions of

salvation. Now, who is it that limits the death of Christ? Why, you. You say that Christ did not die so as infallibly to secure the salvation of anybody. We beg your pardon, when you say we limit Christ's death; we say, 'No, my dear sir, it is you that do it.' We say Christ so died that He infallibly secured the salvation of a multitude that no man can number, who through Christ's death not only may be saved, but are saved, must be saved and cannot by any possibility run the hazard of being anything but saved.

There is only one sense in which it may be said that we limit the grace of God: that is, that we deny that all men individually will be saved. And in this sense, we are not ashamed to put the same limits on grace that God Himself has put, for Universalism is quite contrary to the Scriptures.

Particular atonement would invalidate the universal promises of the Gospel.

God's promises are indeed sincere and given to all. But they express the connection between faith and salvation and demonstrate the duty of all men everywhere to repent and believe; they do not express God's purpose to save all men. For the promises of the gospel are conditional – on willingness to come, on repentance, on belief, on calling on the name of the Lord – but God's purposes are unconditional.

There is thus no contradiction, either in logic or in Scripture or in fact, between particular atonement and God's universal offer of salvation.

The atonement cannot be spoken of in numerical terms.

It is said that we who believe in a particular atonement are trying to tie down to finite terms what is infinite. The atonement was a redemptive act so great that it is meaningless to think of atonement being made for some and not for others.

Everyone will admit that Christ's death is limited in some ways: He did not die for the evil angels, for example. There is, therefore, no reason why it should be meaningless to limit the atonement to those whom God has actually purposed to save.

Far from being meaningless, particular atonement is set forth in the types of the Old Testament dispensation. For example, on the day of atonement, Aaron and his high priestly successors were to make an atonement for the children of Israel for all their sins (*Lev.* 16:34). Here was a particular atonement, made for God's chosen people, and not for the heathen nations round about. The Passover lamb was similarly slain for the Israelites, not for the Egyptians: it was those individuals for whom the blood had been shed who found they were under no condemnation.

The atonement is sufficient for all.

This I do not deny. Owen says: 'The value, worth, and dignity of the ransom which Christ gave Himself to be, and of the price which He paid, was infinite and immeasurable; fit for the accomplishing of any end and the procuring of any good, for all and every one for whom it was intended, had they been millions of men more than ever were created.'

The atonement is sufficient in itself for all those for whom it is intended. If the Lord had intended to save every man, the atonement would be sufficient for it. But in fact He has designed and made this atonement specifically for those whom He actually intends to save by it.

If the atonement is particular, then evangelists can no longer preach that 'Christ died for you'.

This is true, and I believe such a statement to be quite without warrant when addressed to sinners in general. It is no part of the biblical gospel, or of the preaching of the apostles, to say 'Christ died for *you*' – an assertion which is presumptuous on the part both of the one who makes it and of the one who accepts it, who yet may not have saving faith. As J. I. Packer says:

> The fact is that the New Testament never calls on any man to repent on the ground that Christ died specific-ally and particularly for him. The basis on which the New Testament invites sinners to put faith in Christ is simply that they need Him, and that He offers Him-self to them, and that those who receive Him are promised all the benefits that His death secured for His people. What is universal and all-inclusive in the New Testament is the invitation to faith, and the promise of salvation to all who believe . . . The gospel is not, 'Believe that Christ died for everybody's sins, and therefore for yours,' any more than it is, 'Believe that Christ died only for certain people's sins, and so perhaps not for yours.' The gospel is, 'Believe on the

Lord Jesus Christ, who died for sins, and now offers you Himself as your Saviour.' This is the message which we are to take to the world. We have no business to ask them to put faith in any view of the extent of the atonement; our job is to point them to the living Christ, and summon them to trust in Him.

Paul was able to say, 'The Son of God . . . loved me, and gave Himself for me' (*Gal.* 2:20), and every true believer who has received assurance of his salvation may also say this. Why? Because he knows God has *saved* him. No-one who has not *first* repented and trusted in Christ to save him, may legitimately believe that Christ died for him personally.

5

The Hope of Glory

Because our salvation is entirely God's work, we can be assured that 'He who has begun a good work in you will complete *it* until the day of Jesus Christ' (*Phil.* 1:6). The promise of the Lord Jesus, which is sure because God's Word is sure and stands for ever, is that those who come to Him will never be cast out, precisely because those who come to Him have been given to Him by the Father (*John* 6:37; compare *1 Pet.* 1:5, *Heb.* 6:17–19, *Prov.* 4:18). This is the precious truth of the *final perseverance* of the saints – that all who have been born again will be eternally saved. This truth should be distinguished from the concept of the 'eternal security of believers', which implies that a man is saved only for as long as he is able to 'hold on' to God by faith, or that there is nothing for the believer to do *but* believe.

The promises of eternal life in the Scriptures are given to those who shall endure, who are faithful even to death, who persevere, who watch and pray (*Matt.* 24:13, *Rev.* 2:10, *James* 1:12, *Matt.* 25:13); and the expression 'final perseverance' reminds the Christian that these things, like the first act of repentance and faith, are gifts from God. It is by the grace of God that the saints persevere to the end (*Psa.* 37:24). The doctrine that a man who has been saved by the blood of Christ, who has been born of the Spirit of God, and in whom the Spirit dwells, could ever fall from grace, is one of the most injurious ever invented. The Word of God flatly denies it; for Christ will never part with the soul for which He paid so dearly with His precious blood. Backslide, like Peter, a man may; leave his first love, like the church at Ephesus, he may; grieve the Holy Spirit he may; but be forsaken by God he cannot; for he has been for ever united with the Lord Jesus in an embrace that can never be broken (*Song of Sol.* 2:16; 8:7). His sins are covered by the blood of the Lamb. The Lord God sees us in our Saviour rather than in our sin.

Scripture makes it clear that saints are elected to salvation through *sanctification* (*2 Thess.* 2:13, *1 Pet.* 1:2), and that the same Holy Spirit who works regeneration also works sanctification (*Ezek.* 36:27, *Rom.* 15:16) in the life of the believer. 'Unsanctified Christian', 'Christian who does not have the Holy Spirit', 'Christian who has only accepted Christ as Saviour and not as Lord', these are all contradictions in terms. Paul clearly writes to the Christians at Corinth, to whom he confessed he could not speak as spiritual but as carnal (*1 Cor.* 3:1, 3), that they (of all people) were sanctified (*1 Cor.* 6:11), that they had received their new life from the Holy Spirit (*2 Cor.* 3:3), that they were temples of the Holy Spirit (*1 Cor.* 6:19) and that if they were born of God's Spirit, then Jesus Christ was their Lord (*1 Cor.* 12:3) as well as their Saviour. Sanctification, as much as election, regeneration and justification, is the work of the Lord. Every one who partakes of these benefits must also partake of sanctification and is a saint in the true sense – a sanctified one, separated to God's service. By God's grace, saints are able to live the consecrated lives of discipleship required of them, because they are living in the strength of the Lord Jesus Christ. As those who have been set free from bondage to sin (*John* 8:36), they are able both to will and to do the things that please God, because such works spring from a living faith in Christ: to work out their own salvation, to put to death the deeds of the body, to seek holiness, without which no-one shall see the Lord, and to abstain from sin (*Phil.* 2:12–13, *Rom.* 8:13, *Heb.* 12:14, *1 Pet.* 2:11). It is by the fruits of the Spirit that Christians are known to be God's children – those sweet fruits of obedience to the Word of God which must follow when the Holy Spirit dwells within a man; for, if anyone is in Christ, he is a *new* creation (*2 Cor.* 5:17). Scripture knows nothing of Christians who show no signs of sanctification (*1 John* 2:19), and one of the signs that sanctification is taking place is a

continual and irreconcilable war, the flesh lusting against the Spirit, and the Spirit against the flesh; in which war, although the remaining corruption may for a time much prevail, yet, through the continual supply of strength from the sanctifying Spirit of Christ, the regenerate part doth overcome; and so the saints grow in grace, perfecting holiness in the fear of God (*Westminster Confession* xiii:2–3).

The glorious work of our salvation finds its completion in the second coming of the Lord Jesus Christ; then takes place the resurrection and glorification of the saints, who will be for ever in the presence of the One who loved them and washed them from their sins (*1 Thess.* 4:16–18, *Rev.* 7:14–17). Our glorification is certain (*John* 6:39–40); and so it is that the saints fight the good fight of faith here below, strengthened by the knowledge that because God directs all things after the counsel of His own will His cause will ultimately triumph. So too, they watch and pray for that great day when death will flee in the face of the glory of the Lord Jesus Christ, when sorrow and sighing shall be no more, when they shall have everlasting joy and when they shall be with Him for ever.

He who testifies to these things says, 'Surely I am coming quickly.' Amen. Even so, come, Lord Jesus.

Questions and Objections Considered

There are several passages which speak of believers falling away: 1 Cor. 8:11, Rom. 14:15, Heb. 6:4–8, Heb. 10: 26–31, 2 Pet. 2:1, 20–22.

The first two scriptures mentioned are similar and may be considered together. Paul says that no cause of stumbling should be put before a weak brother. He explains that this is a sin, because its natural tendency is to cause the weak Christian to fall into sin and to perish, which would be to frustrate the purpose of Christ in dying for him. It is not implied that this could actually happen; it is sufficient that without God's intervention, it would happen. When Saul threw a javelin at David (*1 Sam.* 18:11) he intended to kill him and was guilty, because the intrinsic tendency of his action was to kill; yet it was not possible that he should succeed, for God had anointed David to be King over Israel.

Of the passages in Hebrews there are several possible interpretations. (1) Despite the strong expressions used in Hebrews 6:4–5 and 10:29, many commentators (for example, Calvin and Owen) believe these passages to refer to professing Christians who have been enlightened and have received many of the privileges of God, and yet who are not true believers (for example, King Saul or Judas). They claim that nothing is here said which *must* necessarily be understood of the regenerate. (2) Others consider that it is more natural to understand true believers to be spoken of, but that the cases are hypothetical, intended as a warning. When Paul warned the sailors to stay in the ship (*Acts* 27:31), he explained that unless they stayed they could not be saved. Yet he knew, and had previously told them (verse 22–26), that they would be saved. It was still necessary to warn them not to do what he knew they would not do. God ordains not only ends, but also the means to those ends. The view that these passages in Hebrews 6 and 10 are hypothetical is supported by 6:9, in which the writer makes it clear that he does not think that this will happen to any of his readers; and Hebrews 10:26 begins, 'For if we sin . . .'. This may therefore also legitimately be understood as hypothetical. (3) The interpretation that these passages speak of the actual apostasy of true believers, while possible from these alone, is not necessary, as we have shown, and contradicts the clear testimony of other passages.

The most probable explanation of 2 Peter 2:1 is that Peter is speaking of these false teachers according to the terms of their own profession. They claimed that Jesus was their Lord and Redeemer and were therefore considered as His people by the church. Their denial of Jesus Christ under these circumstances aggravated their condemnation. In general, Scripture ascribes to those in the fellowship of the church that which is strictly applicable only to those who are in fact elect and redeemed.

2 Peter 2:20 speaks of a reformation from the ways of the world, which may be merely outward, and this is confirmed by verse 22. The sow that is washed is outwardly clean – but it is still a *sow*: its nature is unchanged, and it is for this reason that it returns to wallow in the mire. The unregenerate man may, by close contact with the gospel, reform his conduct and behave like a Christian; but his nature is the same, and he inevitably returns to his sinful ways.

God will not force me to continue to be a Christian against my will.

This objection is similar to the objection that it is possible to resist the Holy Spirit, and it contains a contradiction; for, when the Spirit of God brings a soul to new birth, a new principle is planted within that person, the work of God within him 'both to *will* and to do for His good pleasure'. Anyone who does not will to continue to confess Christ and who does not want to become like Him – who looks back and falls away – can never have truly belonged to the Lord Jesus Christ and is not an inheritor of the kingdom of God. In the continual warfare between the flesh and the Spirit, the flesh may for a time gain the upper hand, and the believer may backslide. This is plain both from Scripture and from Christian experience. However, the regenerate nature, the will and the desire to please God and to abide in Christ, can never be vanquished and one day will overcome all, by the grace of God, who restores the soul, and who freely and abundantly forgives.

Peter, the backsliding believer, wept tears of godly sorrow and repentance, when he saw his sin. Judas, the apostate, filled with remorse when he saw what his action had led to, went out and committed the sin which admits of no repentance by hanging himself. The one, who had been granted saving faith in the Lord Jesus, was restored; the other, who had never possessed true faith, was cast out.

The doctrine of the final preservation of Christians leads logically to the supposition that the saved can live as they please, since they can never be lost.

This is precisely how those professing Christians known as antinomians reasoned. Their licentious and utterly immoral behaviour brought shame and dishonour upon the name of Christ and caused many saintly men to react sharply against any doctrine teaching eternal and assured salvation for anybody on this earth. Like the previous objection, this one embraces the same contradiction and ignores the fact that the Christian, the true believer, is a *changed* person – he no longer desires the things the world desires, nor reasons as the world reasons. His desire is to become holy, to glorify God by walking in the steps of his Master, to hate sin in all its forms, and to flee from it and from all occasions of temptation for all that his soul is worth. The logic which infers the legitimacy of immorality from the truth of final perseverance is false logic. It ignores the fact that the same Spirit who preserves also *sanctifies* and transforms. 'Without holiness, no-one will see the Lord'; no-one who uses his 'knowledge' of eternal salvation as a cloak for mischief can have any reason to believe that he is one of God's elect. 'Let him who thinks he stands take heed lest he fall.'

6

Another Gospel

Many who have read thus far may well feel that they do not recognize the gospel with which they are familiar in what has been said. It is my contention that there is a real and basic difference between the biblical gospel of our Lord Jesus Christ and the prevailing man-made substitute. To substantiate this claim, I must examine the modern gospel and compare it with Scripture, for our final authority must be Scripture alone, where we find many warnings against false gospels (for example *Gal.* 1:6–9, *1 Tim.* 6:3, 20, *2 Tim.* 1:13–14). If we are to be true to our duty to 'Test all things; hold fast what is good' (*1 Thess.* 5:21), we must test all formulations of the gospel against the one true gospel revealed in the Word of God.

If the gospel commonly preached today is indeed found to be unscriptural, it follows that much of modern evangelicalism has gone astray on doctrines which are not just of secondary importance, but are at the heart of the Christian faith. This is not a welcome conclusion, but we must not avoid it for that reason. In the last few years the Lord has laid a desire for the revival of true, deep, vital and powerful Christianity on the hearts of many. It may well be that the recovery of the purity of the gospel will, by the grace of God, lead to a healing of the many ills and weaknesses of the evangelical churches and to a demonstration of the Holy Spirit's power amongst us both in the growth in grace of believers and in the salvation of the lost.

I am convinced that much modern preaching which purports to be evangelical falls short of scriptural teaching and has little in common with the example of the Master Evangelist, the Lord Jesus Christ Himself. How would much modern evangelistic preaching and writing answer the question of the rich young ruler, 'What must I do to inherit life?'? The following answer is probably typical: 'If I am to benefit from Christ's death I must take three simple steps, of which the first two are preliminary, and the third so final that it will make me a Christian: I must believe that I am, in God's sight, a sinner, that is, *I must admit my need*; I must *believe that Christ died for me*; I must *come to him*, and claim my personal share in what He did for everybody.' Under the third and final step is explained how the willing sinner must 'open the door of his heart to Christ', the Christ who waits patiently outside the door until we open it to Him.

It is undeniable that such an answer, or something like it, is frequently presented today, and those who use this method probably justify it by claiming that it includes the central doctrines of the gospel –

repentance, faith, conversion, substitutionary atonement, the sinfulness of man, and so on. If someone
'takes the step' but later questions the validity of his
conversion, he is assured, '*You* took a simple step,
you committed yourself to Jesus Christ, but *then* God
performed a stupendous miracle. He gave you new
life; you were born again.' The concluding advice is
often given: 'Tell somebody today what you have
done.' This answer bears little resemblance to Jesus'
reply to the rich young ruler (*Mark* 10:17–22).

The following is a summary of some of the basic
doctrines or presuppositions of this modern gospel:

Unregenerate men can repent and believe.

Christ died for the sins of every man individually.

*Committing oneself to Christ, or deciding for Him,
or coming to Him, is an act which the sinner can do
as he wills at any time; that is, it is an act of free will.*

*Although God may be said to have taken the initi-
ative in a general sense by sending Christ to die to
make salvation possible, in any particular conversion
it is the sinner who takes the initiative by coming to
Christ, and it is God who responds.*

Now let us compare these doctrines with the teaching
of scripture:

*The unregenerate man cannot believe the gospel,
because it is foolishness to him; spiritual truths are
spiritually discerned, and he lacks the requisite
faculty, being spiritually dead in trespasses and sins
(1 Cor. 1:18; 2:14, Eph. 2:1).*

It follows that he must be born again (which is the sovereign act of God) before he can repent and believe. Faith in Christ is the gift of God. Thus salvation is wholly of the Lord; He takes the initiative (John 3:3–8, Phil. 1:6, 29, Jon. 2:9, 1 Pet. 1:2).

There is no gospel command in Scripture to believe that Christ died for *your* sins. No-one can have legitimate assurance of this until he has been saved and can make his 'calling and election sure' by wholehearted trust and obedience. Rather, the gospel command is to repent and believe in Christ as the only Saviour, believing his promises and casting oneself on His mercy. We have already seen that Christ died for the elect (or, for those who believe) (*John* 10:11–16; 15:13–14, *Rom.* 5:6–11, *Eph.* 5:25–27, *Heb.* 9:15).

This modern gospel is presented with no hint that God is sovereign and active in drawing to Himself those whom He has chosen. In Scripture these truths are not hidden lest they should cause offence; they are declared and even emphasized, since God is glorified when man can boast of nothing in himself as the cause of salvation. 'I contribute nothing to my salvation except the sin from which I need to be saved' (*Acts* 13:48, *Matt.* 11:25–30, *John* 6:63–65; 15:16, *Rom.* 9:14–24).

It is implied that Christ's death merely made salvation *possible* for all, the salvation becoming actual only on the condition of belief. But the Scriptures without exception speak of Christ's death as actually effective in itself, because of its substitutionary nature, to redeem, reconcile, ransom and save to the uttermost (*Rom.* 5:10, *2 Cor.* 5:21, *Eph.* 2:13, *1 Thess.* 5:9–10, *Heb.* 10:10, *1 Pet.* 1:18–20, *1 John* 4:10, *Rev.* 1:5).

Having examined this new gospel in its essentials and shown that it is not the true gospel of the Bible, I want to show that its subsidiary terms are equally erroneous. These are some examples of the sorts of points that are often made.

The benefits enjoyed by the Christian – joy, peace, fulfilment, meaning in life – are often made the ground of an appeal to the unsaved. This is, of course, a motive well-designed to lead the natural man to 'make a decision' for Christ, but it is misleading when divorced from the preaching of the wrath of God against sin, the need for a complete change of nature and the demand for true repentance, all of which are found in the New Testament gospel.

Jesus is represented as a loving but impotent figure, standing and knocking outside the door of our lives. There is only one door-handle, on the inside, where the sinner alone can control it. The feeling excited is one of pity: 'He has done so much for you; will you not now open the door to Him and allow Him to bless you with His salvation?'

This leads the hearer to feel that he has done God a favour by agreeing to believe! What could be more different from the spirit of the tax-collector in the parable, who dared not approach God but stood afar off and cried in humility and repentance, 'God be merciful to me a sinner'?

This is what the modern gospel says. Equally important is what it does *not* say. Jesus' answer to the rich young ruler who asked what he must do to inherit eternal life was: 'You know the commandments' (*Mark* 10:19), thus pointing him to the holiness of God to show him his sinfulness. The failure to preach God's law and the depth of man's sinfulness and guilt is responsible for the evident lack of true conviction of sin in the souls of so many who profess conversion. Furthermore, it leads sinners to believe that there is no need of a change of nature which it is not within their power to effect. 'To be incessantly telling a sinner to "come to Christ" is of little use, unless you tell him why he needs to come, and show him fully his sins' (J. C. Ryle). The modern evangelist often seems to proceed as if unaware of texts like 'Without holiness no-one will see the Lord' (*Heb.* 12:14).

Secondly, what the modern gospel *does* say about sin, repentance and faith is too often a weakened version of what Scripture says. There are probably very few who would not be willing to 'admit their need'. But is 'admitting one's need' the same thing as repentance? True repentance is much more than 'saying sorry'. The word literally means 'a change of mind', a determination to turn away from all those things which we know to be wrong in our lives, and a willingness to go God's way. Furthermore, is believing that Jesus Christ died for sinners all that is involved in faith? On this basis, the very devils are believers! Real saving faith in Christ is much more than an intellectual assent to the truths of the gospel. It means a personal trust and dependency on Christ as the one who paid the penalty for sinners on the cross. It is to be feared that many are taught to believe that they are saved when in fact they are still in their sins.

Thirdly, is it wise to lay stress on how easy it is to become a Christian? It is true that the grace of God is free, yet Scripture exhorts us to *strive* to enter the kingdom, to lay hold of God while He may be found, to examine our souls, to seek the grace of God, to repent of and forsake our sinful ways. Did not Jesus say that the gate is narrow and the way is difficult that leads to life? Let it never be forgotten, however, that sinners *cannot* come to repentance and faith unless grace is given to them by God. One of the mischiefs of much modern evangelism is that it speaks as if conversions could be manufactured at man's pleasure. Accordingly, as man is in full control, and as it is all 'up to him', this type of preaching seeks to bring it within the power of all to be born again, merely by sincerely echoing the evangelist's closing prayer. Does this not resemble the Roman Catholic doctrine of grace conferred '*ex opere operato*', mechanically, by the works of man?

In this kind of preaching, there is a movement away from a heart transaction with God towards the performance of an outward act. This is the danger of an invitation to stand up or sign a decision card, or even to pray a suggested prayer of commitment. The problem is that men and women can go through a form of words and yet never truly repent of their sins or put their trust in Christ. But then, on the basis of having prayed such a prayer or come forward at the close of a meeting, the sinner is often told, '*You* did this, therefore Christ has come into your life. You are definitely a Christian, and if you doubt it, that is tantamount to doubting the very words of Christ Himself.'

This particular methodology can so easily give false assurance to sinners who have never truly come to Christ in repentance and faith. Moreover, it can have the serious effect of inoculating them against the true gospel. How sad it is when one hears folk say, 'I've tried Christianity: I made a commitment to Christ, but it didn't work.' The reality is that such people never encountered the gospel of the New Testament in the first place. Instead they were presented with a man-made substitute which in truth does not work!

Surely we must encourage our hearers not to trust in any outward act, not even in saying a particular prayer, as a guarantee of eternal salvation. The emphasis must always be on the heart transaction with God. And so the questions that we must ask are these: 'Have you truly repented of your sins? Are you trusting in Jesus as the One who alone can save sinners through His death on the cross?' To all such the Lord says, 'I will never cast you out. I will never turn you away.'

In making the above comments, I am not condemning the practice of encouraging interested enquirers to stay behind for counselling at the end of a meeting.

But the danger is to confuse the act of staying behind with the reality of true conversion. That we must never do.

What then is our conclusion? There is today, as there has been in other periods of history, a gospel which looks plausibly like the biblical gospel but which differs from it in several vital respects. We must give no place to this but, like Paul, ensure that the truth of the gospel remains with us (*Gal.* 2:5).

7

Our Attitudes

Ourselves

What is the effect of the biblical gospel on the individual in living the Christian life? In this section, I want to attempt an answer, but without introspectively focusing attention on our individual spiritual lives. My aim throughout is to turn attention away from what man does and the position he takes, and to look instead at who God is and what He has done, is doing, and will do.

From this, certain inferences about man's position and status will be obvious, and certain other things will be apparent about the nature of our responsibilities to other Christians, to the non-Christian world and to individuals all around us. So, in this chapter, I am not in the least intending to be exhaustive or even original. I merely wish to highlight a few points in the hope that they will, firstly, show that the doctrine I have set out is not conceived in the abstract alone nor divorced from practical experience; secondly, indicate some areas of experience where Christians are finding difficulty and where the doctrines outlined may help towards solutions; and thirdly, stimulate thought and prayer and, above all, a God-centred life.

This last, indeed, is the crux of what I wish to say. 'No longer I . . . but Christ', wrote Paul (*Gal.* 2:20). The whole passage is worth quoting because it shows up basic weaknesses which result from some of the ideas that are currently in fashion: 'I have been crucified with Christ; it is no longer I who live, but Christ lives in me; and the *life* which I now live in the flesh I live by faith in the Son of God, who loved me and gave Himself for me. I do not set aside the grace of God; for if righteousness *comes* through the law, then Christ died in vain.' If only we all believed *that*, and lived by it! But, instead, many have slipped into the attitude that, really, our turning to God was rather a kind favour. We committed ourselves to Him as a recognition of some need in our lives, rather like one businessman doing a 50–50 deal with another: as a sort of gentleman's agreement, with both sides pleased and satisfied.

Not so Paul! 'Crucified with Christ' – 'I no longer live, but Christ' – Paul knew only too well that the Christian life does *not* consist of a man's going full steam ahead with good works for Christ in his own strength. On the contrary, it is Christ who dwells within the heart of man, providing the motive and power for all that he does. This is the crucial difference between the 'works' which Paul insists are not part of our salvation (*Eph.* 2:9) and those which James says are (*James* 2:24). The former are the works which we misguidedly do to try to earn our fellowship with God, and the latter are those that proceed, as day follows the dawn, from the indwelling and motivating Holy Spirit. It is only as we are found in Christ that we are able to do *anything* good at all (*John* 15:5).

These are terrible and uncomfortable truths for us to stomach, for the obvious reason that, when we realize them fully, they make us feel small. But the fact that we find this to be so shows the truth of what we have been trying to show – that we have far too high an opinion of ourselves. Humility is the quality we so often pray for and so earnestly wish was not required of us. Yet to realize, even in part, the amazing holiness of God, the horrible sinfulness of man, and then the love that searched us out and *gave* us free pardon, life and glory can only make us grateful and thankful, unspeakably so. The reaction *cannot* be: 'Well, having looked at all the evidence and given the matter my sober and rational consideration, I will commit myself to this person who is being spoken of.' To state it this way – and it is uncomfortably close to some current attitudes – reveals at once the arrogance of the human heart.

When we realize our total debt to Christ we shall again be on the joyful path the apostles took, a tiny group facing the world with the gospel. We will join the Reformers in their joy in holding to the truth, and in their holy zeal, which led some even to the stake. We will join those many faithful servants of the Lord who have willingly given up comfort, prestige and security to go to the ends of the earth for the One who died for them. There will be no sense of 50–50 partnership between man and God and little of the consequent lukewarm or self-induced 'spirituality' which is all too common today. If the gospel were fully understood, who would ever worry whether commitment to Christ might mean having to do a lot of things we might find uncomfortable? If men and women realize that Christ has delivered their souls from death (*Psa.* 116:8), they will also trust Him to deliver their 'eyes from tears, and [their] feet from falling'. These things are secondary. The need for salvation is so great that whatever service, whatever difficulties come with it, they should be thought of no account compared with 'the excellence of the knowledge of Christ Jesus my Lord' (*Phil.* 3:8). Indeed, as the rest of that passage shows, we should look at it the other way round and count *all* things as loss for this, rejoicing rather to share suffering with Christ.

How far most of us seem from this ideal which is the biblical pattern, and the one which in every generation has marked out those Christians who live by the teaching of the Bible! Yet we are not so far off as to be unable to be drawn close. The remedy is clear from the principles we have already given. Paul's teaching in his letter to the Philippians is especially relevant here.

Finally, we are not left on our own with regard to the future. The partnership idea which I have been talking of, and which may be familiar to many present-day Christians, results very easily in the person concerned looking at his future, 'thinking it all out for himself', settling it with himself whom he is to marry, what job he is to get, where he is to live, and so on; and finally taking the attitude: 'Well, this seems to be working out, therefore it must be the Lord's will.' If we believe Ephesians 2:8 and 9, let us also rejoice in verse 10: 'For we are His workmanship, created in Christ Jesus for good works, which God prepared beforehand that we should walk in them.' The application is obvious, though it is very wide, covering the largest areas of life and the smallest too. 'You are not your own. For you were bought at a price' (*1 Cor.* 6:19, 20).

This whole subject is too large for our present scope. The bibliography suggests further reading on these and related topics. It is mentioned in outline, however, to show that in this area too there is a need for the revitalizing which a fresh and right awareness of God's sovereignty will give. It will have applications in the areas of personal devotional life and behaviour and in corporate Christianity. It will take effect in one's vocation and whole life-work. But with the foundation right, the whole building will develop as the Lord wills it to do: 'You are God's field, God's building' (*1 Cor.* 3:9).

Other Christians

The fact of God's great love, free and undeserved, has very definite application in our relationships with others. One of the classic biblical expressions of this is found in 1 John 4:7–12: 'Beloved, let us love one another; for love is of God, and everyone who loves is born of God, and knows God. He who does not love does not know God: for God is love. In this the love of God was manifested towards us, that God has sent His only begotten Son into the world, that we might live through Him. In this is love, not that we loved God, but that He loved us, and sent His Son to be the propitiation for our sins. Beloved, if God so loved us, we also ought to love one another. No-one has seen God at any time. If we love one another, God abides in us and His love has been perfected in us.'

This passage shows quite clearly the chain of reasoning required. God has loved us without our deserving it: when, therefore, He 'comes and makes His home with us' (see *John* 14:23), it must follow that we love one another. We assent to this certainly, yet the fact that our love for one another is often cold and at best spasmodic is all too clear from experience. With the passage from John's epistle in mind, we find ourselves asking whether we fail because we have lost sight of the great love with which *God first loved us* (*Eph.* 2:4). When we again see our unworthiness and God's free love, we shall be on the road to loving one another, not 'in word or in tongue, but in deed and in truth' (*1 John* 3:18).

Another basic application of the gospel of grace is the need for humility. We all know of this and acknowledge our lack, and yet we may aim at it in the wrong way. We approach it sometimes as if it were something *we* achieved: 'Humility and how I achieved it.' We have to learn that humility is the state of realizing that we *are* nothing and can *do* nothing by ourselves that will be of any use at all. Since that realization is one of the basic presuppositions of the whole gospel of grace, may it not be that our own lack of humility again underlines the fact that we are in danger of losing sight of this gospel? Humility is the state of one who realizes that he is not just inadequate for life, or restless, or purposeless, but totally sinful and unworthy, and who realizes his dependence on God for everything. If we realize afresh all that was done for our salvation (see especially Phil. 2:1–11), can we *fail* to be humbled? We enter the state of humility through the door of humiliation and it is, alas, to this that we put up some of our strongest, most foolish and most obstinate barriers.

I now turn to apply what has been said to communal Christian living, on the basis of general principles drawn from Scripture.

First, then, we are to live in loving fellowship with one another. On what is this based? Note, first, that it cannot and must not rest on any foundation of common culture or race, intellectual or social background, or any such human basis. It is to our shame that so much that passes today for Christian fellowship is, in fact, a happy consensus of people on one or other of these bases. Think of the effect when a Christian enters who does not share the basis in question. Like the theology about which I am expressing concern, this is man-centred and shows all the fruits of this basic misconception. Lack of love, sympathy, openness and honesty in a fellowship, and the presence of petty squabbling and bickering, are all tell-tale symptoms of the basic man-centredness of much that passes for Christian fellowship today.

What, then, is our basis to be? Surely, the things all Christians have in common: their awareness of their own unworthiness, their having been snatched out of the fire by a loving heavenly Father; their participation in the Holy Spirit; their membership of the Body of Christ in their new status as children of God; and their common heritage as heirs of eternal life and glory (*Zech.* 3:2, *Phil.* 2:1, *1 Cor.* 12:12, *Rom.* 8:16, *Titus* 3:7). Of these points one in particular is vital for a true understanding of the *basis* of fellowship: membership of the Body of Christ. As family love, ideally, exists among those who share common parentage, so Christian love should be in evidence among those who are brothers and sisters as children of God. Thus love is not just 'the best way of living together for the sake of peace and quiet'; it is the characteristic state of the family of God, who is Himself love in all its fullness.

It would be a long task (though a thrilling one) to describe how this works out in practice but space does not permit. Chapter 13 of 1 Corinthians is an excellent starting point, and most of us would find that verses 4 to 7 set a very high standard if we determined to put them into practice:

Love suffers long and is kind; love does not envy; love does not parade itself, is not puffed up; does not behave rudely, does not seek its own, is not provoked, thinks no evil; does not rejoice in iniquity, but rejoices in the truth; bears all things, believes all things, hopes all things.

Our lives must become a visible expression of these principles as we walk together in the light (see *1 John* 1), open and honest with one another, and praying for each other in all these things – for exhortation without prayer will prove to be of little spiritual value.

Finally, what is fellowship aiming at? True fellowship will be of great value in personal comfort, encouragement, and strength to all that belong. If one member suffers, what do the others do (*1 Cor.* 12:26)? Do they pretend they have not noticed and show their embarrassment in silence? Surely, they suffer together, and weep with those that weep as much as they rejoice with those that rejoice (*Rom.* 12:15). As we remind ourselves of the example of the early church (*Acts* 4:32–35), the contrast with our own attitude becomes uncomfortably apparent. It is all too easy for western Christians to live in luxury, hardly giving a thought for their brethren suffering for the faith in Muslim lands and elsewhere. This principle is as wide as the world in application and as minute in detail as a fellowship of 'two or three'. Let us practise it and rejoice to do so.

But all this is the secondary purpose of fellowship. What is the main purpose of our love? Christ said, 'By this all will know that you are My disciples, if you have love for one another' (*John* 13:35). What a challenge and responsibility! The warmth of a genuine Christian fellowship is one of the most attractive things in the world, beyond the charm of the individual personality or the fascinating depths of intellectual discussion. Let us test ourselves:

Would the outsider, stumbling on a Bible study group, appreciate that he had come face to face with people who loved each other in deed and in truth (*1 John* 3:18)? Or would he find a group of individuals determined to express their point of view, to win arguments, to hold supposed truth and forget love? We are none of us guiltless, and no stones are cast. But that is no reason for not attempting to put right things that are wrong.

Love is evidently a quality which exhortation can do precious little to produce – which is just as well! We must again come to the Lord and Giver of life and confess that we are incapable of it ourselves. Then, as we seek Him in prayer and in His Word, and as He richly pours out His Spirit upon us, we shall begin to find the fruits of the Spirit becoming apparent – like the wind, without a visible starting point. And the first of these fruits is the amazing and treasured love that we long to see more and more in ourselves and in the Body of Christ throughout the world. Once again, we are powerless. Let us then turn to Him who is Power and Love and seek in Him all we lack.

Evangelism

The Lord has declared His will in the Holy Scriptures, and the central message of the Scriptures is the gospel. We have seen what that gospel is: It is the good news of salvation by grace, for the Lord Jesus Christ has redeemed His people. But the Church of Jesus Christ has been entrusted with this glorious good news, and we are not to keep it to ourselves. We have also been given the task of evangelism, which is simply to declare the gospel to the world. Just as God has given the good news to us, we are to pass it on to others; for this is God's means of bringing men and women to salvation – the preaching and hearing of the gospel.

Evangelism is not persuading people to make a decision; it is not proving that God exists or making out a good case for the truth of Christianity; it is not inviting someone to a meeting; it is not exposing the contemporary dilemma or arousing interest in Christianity; it is not wearing a badge saying 'Jesus Saves'! Some of these things may be right and good in their place, but none of them should be confused with evangelism. To evangelize is to declare on the authority of God what He has done to save sinners, to warn men of their lost condition, to direct them to repent, and to believe in the Lord Jesus Christ. Richard Baxter gives some valuable directions for this task:

> We must take all opportunities we possibly can to instruct them how to attain salvation. If the person be ignorant, labour to make him understand the chief happiness of man, how far he was once possessed of it; the covenant God then made with him; how he broke it; what penalty he incurred; and what misery he brought himself into: teach him his need of a Redeemer; how Christ did mercifully interpose, and bear the penalty; what the new covenant is; how men are drawn to Christ; and what are the riches and privileges which believers have in him. If he is not moved by these things, then show him the excellency of the glory he neglects; the extremity and eternity of

the torments of the damned; the justice of enduring them for wilfully refusing grace; the certainty, nearness, and terrors of death and judgment; the vanity of all things below; the sinfulness of sin; the preciousness of Christ; the necessity of regeneration, faith and holiness, and the true nature of them. If, after all, you find him entertaining false hopes, then urge him to examine his state; show him the necessity of doing so; help him in it; nor leave him till you have convinced him of his misery and remedy. Show him how vain and destructive it is to join Christ and his duties, to compose his justifying righteousness. Yet be sure to draw him to the use of all means; such as hearing and reading the Word, calling upon God, and associating with the godly; persuade him to forsake sin, avoid all temptations to sin, especially evil companions, and to wait patiently on God in the use of means, as the way in which God will be found.

Our motives for evangelism are important, for if they are not scriptural motives our evangelism may become distorted or cold, and God will not honour a self-centred evangelist.

False motives are very dangerous and subtle, and liable to deceive us as well as others. It is all too possible for selfishness to be the driving force. One may evangelize in order to boost his self-esteem by 'bringing someone through' as the phrase goes, or in order to keep up with the Joneses spiritually, or to feel important in the service of God. We need to examine ourselves concerning these matters in the light of God's Word and to repent and come to Him for cleansing.

What were the factors which motivated the first century Christians in their desire to declare the good news of the gospel?

In the first place, they had a command, a Great Commission, from the Lord Himself. Jesus said, 'Go therefore and make disciples of all the nations' (*Matt.* 28:19). That command has never been revoked. It has been well said that the sovereignty of God is expressed in His commands as much as in His decrees. Because He is our sovereign Lord, when He commands we must obey. Evangelism therefore is not an optional extra. We all have a God-given responsibility to tell others the good news.

Secondly, they were indebted to Christ for all that He had done for them. The Apostle Paul said, 'For the love of Christ compels us' (*2 Cor.* 5:14) As Paul contemplated the amazing love of God in sending Jesus to die upon the cross, he was so filled with wonder and gratitude that he was prepared to go to the ends of the earth for the sake of the One who had done so much for him. C. T. Studd, the famous and wealthy England cricketer, who gave up fame and fortune at the height of his career to become a missionary in China, once said these words: 'If Jesus Christ be God and died for me, no sacrifice can be too great for me to make for Him.'

Thirdly, they were conscious of the eternal issues which were at stake. 'Nor is there salvation in any other, for there is no other name under heaven given among men by which we must be saved' (*Acts* 4:12). One of the reasons why many modern evangelicals have lost their zeal for evangelism is that the doctrine of eternal punishment no longer figures prominently in their thinking. Indeed, some have abandoned the doctrine altogether in favour of the so-called theory of 'annihilationism' which says that hell is merely a state of oblivion. Quite apart from the fact that this pernicious notion is quite unscriptural (*Rev.* 14:11), it has removed one of the greatest motivations for evangelism, namely that without Christ men and women are destined for an eternity of endless torment (*Matt.* 25:46, *Mark* 9:43, 48).

Most unbelievers in the world today would be quite happy to settle for oblivion when they die. In fact, that is what the vast majority believes in anyway. But where is the fear in that? Jesus, on the other hand, said, 'Fear Him who . . . has power to cast into hell' (*Luke* 12:5). There should be a fear of hell, and this should be a vital factor in our evangelism. Do we really believe that outwardly decent and respectable non-Christians are heading for an eternity of weeping and gnashing of teeth? If we did, then surely we would be zealous and passionate in our Christian witness. Would we not be almost beside ourselves with holy fervour as we pleaded with men and women to make their peace with God before it is too late?

I turn now to the question of the results of evangelism. Preaching the gospel is not an end in itself: it is the means God has appointed for the salvation of souls. So the evangelist expects, and ought to expect, that his work will lead to conversions. But here is where a full realization of the sovereignty of God in salvation is so essential for the evangelist, to keep him from pride and in humble reliance on the Lord alone. Thus it was that Paul could say to the Corinthians: 'Who then is Paul, and who is Apollos, but ministers through whom you believed, as the Lord gave to each one? I planted, Apollos watered, but God gave the increase. So then neither he who plants is any thing, nor he who waters, but God who gives the increase' (*1 Cor.* 3:5–7).

Such a reliance will lead us to admit that in ourselves we are quite unfitted for the work of evangelism, for it is a spiritual work. Praise God, the implanting of new life is His work, and even our part is done through Him alone. 'Not that we are sufficient of ourselves to think of anything as being from ourselves, but our sufficiency is from God, who has also made us sufficient as ministers of the new covenant, not of the letter, but of the Spirit; for the letter kills, but the Spirit gives life' (*2 Cor.* 3:5–6).

God's sovereignty is not only the source of our ability, but also the ground of our confidence. How a knowledge of this fact should comfort and strengthen us! I mentioned in a previous chapter that when Paul was in Corinth, he was afraid, because of the opposition of the Jews, but God said to him, 'Do not be afraid, but speak, and do not keep silent; for I am with you, and no one will attack you to hurt you; for I have many people in this city' (*Acts* 18:9–10). God will gather in His elect and no opposition of men or Satan shall prevail against His almighty power. He is 'the Lord of the harvest' (*Matt.* 9:38), to

Whom alone we should look in prayer and in action. When we proclaim the gospel, we proclaim the Word of the Lord; and that Word, as it is applied by the Holy Spirit to the hearts of men, has great power. So Peter says: those who have been saved are 'born again, not of corruptible seed, but of incorruptible, through the word of God which lives and abides forever' (*1 Pet.* 1:23).

If, as we have seen, salvation is not of the free-will of man, but of God, it follows that the results of evangelism are entirely from the Lord's hand and according to His will. Therefore we should not be surprised when some hear and accept the gospel, while others reject it. God has promised (and His promises are sure):

> For as the rain comes down, and the snow from heaven,
> And do not return there,
> But water the earth,
> And make it bring forth and bud,
> That it may give seed to the sower
> And bread to the eater,
> So shall My word be that goes forth from My mouth:
> It shall not return to Me void,
> But it shall accomplish what I please,
> And it shall prosper *in the thing* for which I sent it'
> (*Isa.* 55:10–11).

These words indicate that God's word does exactly what He has decreed: nothing more, nothing less. When a group of people hear the gospel, those whom it pleases God to call at that time believe, having been elected to salvation; those whom God passes over and rejects harden their hearts against the gospel and are confirmed in their sinful rebellion. So the ministers of the gospel are 'to God the fragrance of Christ among those who are being saved and among those who are perishing. To the one we are the aroma of death *leading* to death, and to the other the aroma of life *leading* to life. And who is sufficient for these things?' (2 *Cor.* 2:15–16). We are in awe to think that every presentation of the gospel has such a spiritual and eternal effect on the souls of all those who hear: to death, or to life.

It is, of course, true that some who are awakened under gospel preaching afterwards go back, and a consideration of the results of evangelism would be incomplete without facing the question of the genuineness of those results. We must sadly conclude, from Scripture and from experience, that not all who at first appear to be saved are truly born again. 'Our Lord's parable of the sower implies that, however good the seed might be, and careful the sower, there would be stony-ground hearers, and thorny-ground hearers, going a certain length and then turning back. So the backslidings complained of are such as the apostles experienced, and such as our Lord led us to anticipate under the preaching of His own full gospel' (Horatius Bonar). So, if some supposed converts prove not to be genuine, the preacher is not necessarily to be blamed, though this provides no excuse for preaching in such a way as to encourage false professions.

In the light of all that has been said, what should be our methods of evangelism? Here, as in all things, our only rule and guide must be the Holy Scriptures. No pragmatic justification is valid before God.

First, and perhaps self-evidently, our evangelism should be an accurate presentation of the true gospel. It should be complete; it should be balanced – every point given the same emphasis and importance that Scripture gives it; and it should be free from errors. We must not hide the unpalatable parts of the gospel, such as the wrath of God against sin. Such truth always arouses opposition, but God can remove it. Like Paul, let us renounce 'the hidden things of shame, not walking in craftiness nor handling the word of God deceitfully, but by manifestation of the truth commending ourselves to every man's conscience in the sight of God' (2 Cor. 4:2).

Secondly, our evangelism should be openly grounded in the Bible. It is quite possible to present an accurate summary of the gospel in one's own words. But how much more honouring to God, how much more effective, to show directly from the Bible that these things are not the opinions of men but the authoritative declarations of God. 'For the word of God *is* living and powerful, and sharper than any two-edged sword, piercing even to the division of soul and spirit, and of joints and marrow, and is a discerner of the thoughts and intents of the heart' (*Heb.* 4:12).

Thirdly, the non-essentials should not detract from the essentials. There are many forms of communication which can be used today. Most of these are quite unobjectionable in themselves, but there is in many cases a danger of the real gospel message becoming lost in the trimmings. This can be so with Christian songs, or some Christian radio and television programmes, or attempts to give a Christian analysis of modern culture.

Fourthly, we must never forget that preaching the gospel is communication with real people and that their individual characteristics must be taken into account. Thus the preacher will adapt his vocabulary and style (though not the basic content of what he says) to his audience, and the missionary will live with the people of the country to which he goes, as far as possible adopting their way of life and removing unnecessary cultural barriers.

Let us take a brief survey of various kinds of evangelism and apply to them some of these principles.

The evangelism which is most familiar to many Christians is the preaching of the gospel in an evangelistic meeting, whether a church service, a Christian Union meeting, an open-air meeting or a vast 'crusade' meeting. These provide opportunities for many non-Christians at one time to hear the gospel in conditions ideal to gain their full attention to what is said, and with the possibility afterwards to discuss the message with Christians who are present. However, there are dangers which must be avoided. The preacher may easily draw attention to himself rather than to Christ. He may do harm by misleading statements or emphases, or by an emotional 'decisionism' which encourages professions of faith from those in whose hearts there is no saving grace at work. The Lord's name may even be dishonoured by anecdotes which are inappropriate to the gospel. Evangelistic meetings themselves, of course, do not necessarily involve these dangers, but these are abuses which ought to be guarded against, while every opportunity of benefiting the souls of men should be seized.

'Therefore those who were scattered went everywhere preaching the word' (*Acts* 8:4). There is a great need in these days for ordinary Christians to regain this ministry of the early church – every believer a witness for Christ. Let us be found faithful servants in thus spreading the Word of God. If we know and love the Lord, let us also have a thorough knowledge of the Gospel and prayerfully seek opportunities to tell our friends and acquaintances of Him. Here the keynotes should be simplicity, spontaneity, and sincerity. A testimony which is Christ-centred and not self-centred can also be very valuable:

> Come *and* hear, all you who fear God,
> And I will declare what He has done for my soul
> (*Psa.* 66:16).

A true and up-to-date testimony will often strike home to the heart. In conversations with friends, a

Christian may be able to sort out problems, to make the gospel clear, and to be a true ambassador for Christ. We must, of course, avoid any pressurizing or fruitless arguments. But as the Holy Spirit leads and enables us, God can use us in this way.

When Luther was imprisoned in the Wartburg, he was given by the Lord the task of translating the Bible into his native German. Dr Merle d'Aubigné comments: 'The reform was no longer in the hand of the reformer. The Bible was brought forward, and Luther withdrew. God shews Himself, and man disappears. The reformer has entrusted the *Book* to the hands of his contemporaries, and each person is now enabled to understand and listen to God Himself.' It is no less true today that the gospel in printed form can be a very effective means of evangelism, and we have a duty and an opportunity to distribute portions of Scripture and all forms of Christian literature which are faithful to the Word of God.

We must not leave the subject of evangelism without speaking of missionary work overseas. Perhaps our greatest need is a combination of a local with a world-wide vision of God's work. The commission for evangelism is world-wide, for the church of Jesus Christ is composed of His elect and redeemed people from all nations, tribes, peoples and languages (*Rev.* 7:9). The gospel is to be preached in all the world for a witness to all nations, and then the end shall come (*Matt.* 24:14). How concerned we should be, therefore, to take part by prayer and giving in this great work of God and, if the Lord calls us, to go as overseas missionaries ourselves.

Perhaps the reader feels, as the writer certainly does, 'Who is sufficient for these things?' It is here that the Scriptures give their sweetest comfort and strongest encouragement: It is not as of ourselves, weak, sinful, rebellious, foolish; but as of God, sovereign, almighty, holy, the ruler of all, that we are to preach the gospel. Christ said: 'All authority has been given to Me in heaven and on earth. Therefore go . . .' (*Matt.* 28:18). Paul could say, 'I can do all things through Christ who strengthens me' (*Phil.* 4:13). Saved and equipped for service by grace, through faith, let us take God at His word and go forward for Him and with Him.

> *But as we have been approved by God to be entrusted with the gospel, even so we speak, not as pleasing men, but God who tests our hearts.*

8

The End of the Gospel: Worship

To the question, 'What is the chief end of man?' the Westminster Shorter Catechism gives the famous answer: 'Man's chief end is to glorify God, and to enjoy Him for ever.' To this simple but profound statement, our hearts, renewed by the Spirit of the living God, utter a heartfelt 'Amen'. Something within us tells us that this rings true. This pre-eminently is the purpose for which God intended man – a purpose which can now be realized as a result of the saving work of the Lord Jesus Christ for us.

In these pages, I have endeavoured to set out what I believe to be the doctrines of the gospel of the grace of God revealed in the Scriptures. But merely to believe in our minds that these doctrines are true is to profess a form of godliness without power. There are, we must sadly admit, those who would agree fully with the doctrinal position embodied in the earlier chapters, and yet whose hearts are cold toward the

Lord Jesus; whose churches are devoid of the presence of the Holy Spirit, the Lord and Giver of life; whose preaching is but philosophical lecturing. With those who say that such people, for all their 'soundness', have understood the *letter* only, and not the *spirit*, of the gospel, I wholeheartedly agree. As Joseph Hart wrote:

> *True religion's more than notion;*
> *Something must be known and felt.*

So I ask this question: how ought an understanding of the doctrines of grace to affect our attitude to God? What will be the effect upon our relationship with our God of the application by the Holy Spirit to our innermost being of these doctrines, and of their being written with letters of fire upon the tables of our hearts?

The effect upon us ought surely to be that we see ourselves as we are — DEBTORS: debtors to the infinite mercy and grace of the God who has wonderfully delivered us. We acknowledge, upon being asked 'How much do you owe my master?' (*Luke* 16:5), that we owe everything to Him. Day by day, as we walk along the path foreordained, as we look back and see how all things have worked together for our good, we become more and more aware of *how much* we owe; but not until the great day when, before the throne of God, we worship in the company of the innumerable hosts of angels, of the church of the first-born enrolled in heaven, of the spirits of just men made perfect, and of Jesus himself, the mediator of the new covenant — not until then shall we fully realize the breadth and height and depth of God's love toward us:

> *When I stand before the throne,*
> *Dressed in beauty not my own;*
> *When I see Thee as Thou art,*
> *Love Thee with unsinning heart;*
> *Then, Lord, shall I fully know,*
> *Not till then, how much I owe.*

In the meantime, we need to pray that God would open our spiritual eyes wider and wider, so that we grasp more and more of all that He has done for us in Christ. This is where a right relationship with God begins, with the realization of our debt to His amazing grace.

There are many basic things that characterize the relationship with God of one who possesses a deep experimental knowledge of the doctrines of the gospel. Let me touch on a few of them.

First and foremost: *he will be a worshipper.* Was it not in order that He might be worshipped that God made man? And when man fell, was it not in order that this purpose might yet be fulfilled that He saved man? The gospel makes rebels into worshippers. Those who once were afar off, enemies of God, have, by the blood of Christ, been brought into the very presence of the King of kings and Lord of lords in order to worship Him. 'Say among the nations, the LORD reigns' (*Psa.* 96:10) cries the Psalmist. And the response He seeks amongst those who hear this message is that they should bow down before His throne, worshipping the LORD in the beauty of holiness (*Psa.* 96:9). This is giving God the glory due to His name. If God is King in Zion, and we are citizens of the heavenly Jerusalem, then nothing less than perfect submission and the worship of our hearts is what God requires of us and what He delights to see. But God not only requires worship of us – He has, in His mercy, made us *fit* to worship Him, having, as it were, mended and returned our broken and rusted harps, making them even more harmonious and brilliant than they were before they were (so it seemed) irretrievably battered by the fall – in order that we might sing the new song of the redeemed people of God (*Rev.* 5:9).

Furthermore, *his worship is a continuing activity*. It begins here below when the burden of his sins is removed; it continues in glory as, perfected in the Lord Jesus Christ, he casts his crown before the throne upon which he sees the One whom previously he had loved, having not seen. The Christian who is a worshipper will, if I may put it in this way, be immediately 'at home' when he arrives at the end of his pilgrimage, heaven itself, for heaven, the place where the worship of God is unceasing, is a prepared place for a prepared people who, by the working of the Holy Spirit in their lives, are being made ready to enter it.

What a change would be effected in our own lives and in our churches if we learned what worshipping in spirit and in truth really means! We speak glibly of 'joy' in the Christian life; but is it the joy of the Psalmist who spoke from experience when he said:

In Your presence *is* fullness of joy;
At Your right hand are pleasures for evermore
(*Psa.* 16:11)

because he had learned to worship? Do we say, with longing in our hearts: 'Blessed are those who dwell in Your house: they will still be praising You' (*Psa.* 84:4)? Do we know what it is to worship night and day as Anna delighted to do (*Luke* 2:36–38)? Many times we read in Scripture of those who could say with Simeon: 'My eyes have seen Your salvation' (*Luke* 2:30) and who, with thankful hearts, *worshipped* – yet how little we know of the joy of such worship ourselves! How important it is that we, for whom so much has been done in salvation, should learn again to bow down before Almighty God, glorifying God in worshipping Him and finding as we do so that worshipping God is the means by which we enjoy Him!

Let us, then, rid ourselves of the idea that Christians should first and foremost be *workers*, and teach the newly converted to become habitual *worshippers*. We need not fear that to do this will result in a lack of evangelism; far from it! A group of worshippers will also be a group of powerful witnesses to the grace of God. These are the Christians whose testimonies convict unbelievers, for they are able to say from the heart, 'Come and listen to what God has done for me.' Gone will be those barren and sad prayer meetings, so often little more than the repetition in shopping-list fashion of 'prayer-needs', and gone will be the supposition that prayer must always be *for* this or that. Gone, too, will be the subconscious attitude which encourages Christians to put more faith in the act of praying than in the one who is the Inspirer and Hearer of all true prayer. Instead, times of prayer will be times when the presence of the Holy Spirit is longed for and sought after, times when we pour out our souls before God and bring before Him in intercessory prayer those things for which He himself has laid a burden on our hearts.

> Whom have I in heaven *but You*?
> And *there is* none upon earth that I desire besides
> You (*Psa.* 73:25).

Let us learn to pray like this, and we shall find to our joy that God will delight to pour down upon us showers of blessing. We shall begin to *prove* the power of prayer, for

> *Prayer makes the darkened cloud withdraw,*
> *Prayer climbs the ladder Jacob saw,*
> *Gives exercise to faith and love,*
> *Brings every blessing from above.*

How much we need to ask the Lord, as did His disciples, to teach us to pray (*Luke* 11:1)!

Intimately bound up with this are three further attitudes which constitute a close walk with God – which indeed could be said to constitute the worship of our lives: *love of God, fear of God and obedience to His Law.* Deuteronomy 10:12–13 sets out wonderfully what it is that God requires of those upon whom He has set His love: it is 'to fear the LORD your God, to walk in all His ways and to love Him, to serve the LORD your God with all your heart and with all your soul, *and* to keep the commandments of the LORD and His decrees which I command you today for your good'. Here is a picture of the ideal Christian life, as far as the Christian's relationship with God is concerned. For it is as we realize in our hearts that the God to whom 'belong heaven, and the heaven of heavens, the earth, with all that is in it' delighted in us sinners and chose us out of all peoples to be to Him a people for His own possession, that we respond to Him in love and adoration, that we learn to fear Him, and consequently to obey Him.

There is so much superficiality and irreverence among us today that it is significant that the scriptural expression 'a God-fearing man' has almost entirely dropped out of use. Why is so much devotional preaching and writing today oriented towards the man-centred sort of question that begins: 'How can I . . . ?'? I would suggest that these things are indications of something radically wrong with much present-day piety, indications that we have not 'seen the Lord, high and lifted up', but only a pale shadow. Let us once become God-centred in our thinking, treating the things of God with the seriousness they deserve, calling Jesus 'Lord, Lord' *and* doing the things He says, 'working out our salvation with fear and trembling', and we shall find that He will visit us individually and corporately working within us that which will please Him.

Finally, the Christian in close communion with His Lord will *await his coming*, for 'the grace of God that brings salvation has appeared to all men, teaching us that, denying ungodliness and worldly lusts, we should live soberly, righteously, and godly in this present age, looking for the blessed hope and glorious appearing of our great God and Saviour Jesus Christ' (*Titus* 2:11–13).

This hope of the appearing of the Lord Jesus Christ and of being with Him in eternity with that multitude which no man can number who have washed their robes in His blood is what gives the Christian courage on this earth, for he knows that this life is but a pilgrimage, a journey in a foreign land. Soon he will be going home to that heavenly country of which he is a citizen (*Phil.* 3:20, *Heb.* 11:13–16). It is often said of Christians that they are 'so heavenly minded that they are no earthly use'. The truth is that the *more* heavenly minded the Christian is (and he is commanded to set his mind on things that are above, *Col.* 3:1–4) the *more* he will be the salt of the earth and the light of the world.

Let us therefore meditate often upon heaven, awaiting in joyful anticipation that time when God will usher us into His glorious presence. Let us fulfil our calling in this world, wherever God would have us to be, whatever He would have us to do, seeking to be found as profitable servants, working faithfully for Him in the light of eternity. And then, in that great day, when the books are opened and the secrets of all hearts are revealed, the Lord Jesus Christ, our incomparable Saviour, whom we shall see face to face in all

His beauty and glory, will call us home with those wonderful and precious words: 'Well done, good and faithful servant; enter into the joy of your Lord' (*Matt.* 25:21, 23).

> *Shout joyfully before the* LORD, *the King . . .*
> *For He is coming to judge the earth.*

Bibliography

An asterisk denotes a work of particular value as an introduction to the subject. Except where indicated, these titles are all available from the Banner of Truth Trust.

Doctrinal

Berkhof, Louis, *Systematic Theology*
Boettner, Loraine, *The Reformed Doctrine of Predestination* (Eerdmans)
De Witt, J. R., *What is the Reformed Faith?*
Edwards, Jonathan, *Freedom of the Will* (Yale)
Hodge, Charles, *Systematic Theology* (James Clarke)
Luther, Martin, *The Bondage of the Will* (James Clarke)
Murray, John, *Commentary on Romans* (Eerdmans)
*Murray, John, *Redemption, Accomplished and Applied*
Owen, John, *The Death of Death in the Death of Christ*

*Pink, A. W., *The Sovereignty of God*
*Seaton, W. J., *The Five Points of Calvinism*
*Sproul, R. C., *Chosen by God* (Scripture Press)
  Westminster Confession of Faith (Free Presbyterian
    Church of Scotland)

Devotional and Evangelistic

*Blanchard, John, *Right with God*
  Bonar, Andrew, *Memoir & Remains of R. M.
    M'Cheyne*
  Bunyan, John, *Prayer*
  Flavel, John, *The Mystery of Providence*
*Hallesby, O., *Prayer* (Inter-Varsity Press)
  Lloyd-Jones, D. M., *Evangelistic Sermons at
    Aberavon*
  Lloyd-Jones, D. M., *Old Testament Evangelistic
    Sermons*
*Newton, John, *Letters*
*Packer, J. I., *Knowing God* (Hodder)
  Packer, J. I., *A Passion for Holiness* (Crossway)
  Ryle, J. C., *Holiness* (James Clarke)
  Whitefield, George, *Select Sermons*

Practical

*Chantry, W. J., *Today's Gospel: Authentic or
    Synthetic?*
  Lloyd-Jones, D. M., *Preaching and Preachers*
    (Hodder)
  MacArthur, J. F., *Ashamed of the Gospel?*
    (Crossway)
*Martin, A. N., *Practical Implications of Calvinism*

Murray, Iain H., *The Forgotten Spurgeon*
*Murray, Iain H., *Spurgeon v. Hyper-Calvinism*
Murray, Iain H., *The Invitation System*
Wells, David F., *The Bleeding of the Evangelical Church*

Historical and Biographical

*Dallimore, A., *Spurgeon*
Dallimore, A., *George Whitefield (2 vols.)*
D'Aubigné, J. H. Merle, *Reformation in England (2 vols.)*
Murray, Iain H., *Jonathan Edwards: A New Biography*
Murray, Iain H., *D. Martyn Lloyd-Jones: The First Forty Years*
Murray, Iain H., *D. Martyn Lloyd-Jones: The Fight of Faith*
Murray, Iain H., *Revival and Revivalism*
*Ryle, J. C., *Christian Leaders of the Eighteenth Century*
Spurgeon, C. H., *Autobiography (2 vols.)*